D1575655

THE HEDGE FUND
HANDBOOK

OTHER TITLES IN THE IRWIN LIBRARY OF INVESTMENT AND FINANCE

Convertible Securities
by John P. Calamos (1-55738-921-7)

Pricing and Managing Exotic and Hybrid Options
by Vineer Bhansali (0-07-006669-8)

Risk Management and Financial Derivatives
by Satyajit Das (0-07-015378-7)

Valuing Intangible Assets
by Robert F. Reilly and Robert P. Schweihs (0-7863-1065-0)

Managing Financial Risk
by Charles W. Smithson (0-7863-0440-5)

High-Yield Bonds
by Theodore Barnhill, William Maxwell, and Mark Shenkman
    (0-07-006786-4)

Valuing Small Business and Professional Practices, 3rd edition
by Shannon Pratt, Robert F. Reilly, and Robert P. Schweihs
    (0-7863-1186-X)

Implementing Credit Derivatives
by Israel Nelken (0-07-047237-8)

The Handbook of Credit Derivatives
by Jack Clark Francis, Joyce Frost, and J. Gregg Whittaker
    (0-07-022588-5)

THE HEDGE FUND HANDBOOK

A Definitive Guide for Analyzing and Evaluating Alternative Investments

STEFANO LAVINIO

McGraw-Hill

New York San Francisco Washington, D.C. Auckland Bogotá
Caracas Lisbon London Madrid Mexico City Milan
Montreal New Delhi San Juan Singapore
Sydney Tokyo Toronto

Library of Congress Cataloging-in-Publication Data

Lavinio, Stefano.
    The hedge fund handbook / by Stefano Lavinio.
        p.   cm.
    ISBN 0-07-135030-6
    1. Hedge funds. I. Title.
    HG4530.L364 1999
    332.64'5—dc21   99-15642
                                         CIP

McGraw-Hill

*A Division of The **McGraw·Hill** Companies*

1 2 3 4 5 6 7 8 9 0 DOC/DOC 9 0 9 8 7 6 5 4 3 2 1 0 9

ISBN 0-07-135030-6

The sponsoring editor for this book was Stephen Isaacs, the editing supervisor was Patricia V. Amoroso, and the production supervisor was Modestine Cameron. It was set in Palatino per the IPROF design specs by Michele Pridmore of the McGraw-Hill Desktop Publishing Unit, Hightstown, NJ.

Printed and bound by R. R. Donnelley & Sons Company.

This publication is designed to provide accurate and authoritative information in regard to the subject matter covered. It is sold with the understanding that the publisher is not engaged in rendering legal, accounting, or other professional service. If legal advice or other expert assistance is required, the services of a competent professional person should be sought.

         —From a declaration of principles jointly adopted by a committee of the American Bar Association and a committee of publishers.

This book is printed on recycled, acid-free paper containing a minimum of 50% recycled de-inked fiber.

McGraw-Hill books are available at special quantity discounts to use as premiums and sales promotions, or for use in corporate training programs. For more information, please write to the Director of Special Sales, McGraw-Hill, 11 West 19th Street, New York, NY 10011. Or contact your local bookstore.

CONTENTS

Chapter 4

Financial Risk and Hedge Funds   33

Chapter 5

Hedge Fund Returns   49

Chapter 6

Hedge Fund Leverage   63

Chapter 7

Detecting Leverage in Hedge Funds   77

Since the early 1990s there has been a growing awareness about hedge funds, both among investment professionals and in the general public. Often called *alternative investments* or *alternative investment vehicles* because their mandates are not restricted to plain equity and fixed-income investments, hedge funds have grown exponentially in both size and number in a very short time. Without a doubt, the benign financial environment since the early 1990s, characterized by soaring financial asset values and increased wealth generated by a rising stock market, has greatly contributed to this growth. In 1990 there were about 70 hedge funds; today there are about 50,000. As the offerings have widened, so have the number of investors entering this field. The notional value of assets under management by these vehicles is presently estimated to be between U.S. $8 and $15 trillion. Along the way, this growth has seen spectacular performances as well as horrifying collapses. David Askin's Granite Capital, Victor Niederhoffer's Global Systems fund, and John Meriwether's long-term capital management are only a few of the best-known disasters of the 1990s.

As this market has grown, so has its complexity, creating a paradox for investors. Much of the growth in financial markets in the late 1980s and the 1990s has been accompanied by the growth, development and use of powerful quantitative methods, sophisticated software, and increasingly powerful computers. At the same time, the tools and methodologies used by the majority of hedge fund investors and advisors, even the most savvy, have remained very primitive. Some of the techniques presently used fail to capture the essence of these vehicles. For these reasons, the methodologies currently used are downright misleading in many cases. In this book we examine how these vehicles operate, zooming in on the key issues regarding their activities. In so doing, we hope to provide the reader with a firm understanding and some useful tools to effectively evaluate the potential benefits and risks of hedge funds.

THE HEDGE FUND HANDBOOK

CHAPTER 1

General Definitions, Functions, and Characteristics of Hedge Funds

DEFINITION AND FUNCTIONS OF HEDGE FUNDS

Hedge funds are investment vehicles structured as either private partnerships or offshore companies (see App. 1 for a general description of hedge funds and their structure). Their stated objective is to generate above-average returns for their investors. As mentioned in the Introduction, because their mandates are not restricted to plain "buy and hold"-commodity, equity, and fixed-income investments, hedge funds are often called *alternative investments* or *alternative investment vehicles.*

Because they are not restricted to buy-and-hold investment strategies, most hedge funds seek to generate their returns by using some or all of the following investment techniques:

- *Short selling.* This strategy involves the sale of borrowed securities (considered overvalued) in the anticipation of making a profit by repurchasing these securities at a lower price and at a later date. The success of this strategy requires the stock of the target company to fall in line with the manager's expectations. It is a complex strategy to execute. It requires not only the ability to identify overvalued securities but also the ability to cost-efficiently borrow the overpriced stock (to deliver against the original sale) and the ability to productively invest the cash obtained from the original sale. Rising markets, regulatory restrictions on short sales, short squeezes and the leverage often inherent in this technique make it complex to manage successfully as a stand-alone investment technique. Short selling can be, and frequently is, used as a hedging technique (see the following paragraph).

- *Hedging.*   This strategy involves the mitigation of some or all of the risk inherent in a position. Some of these risks include, but are not limited to, economic risk, currency risk, interest rate risk, political risk, market risk, and company risk. Hedging entails costs that can erode investment performance if used excessively or implemented incorrectly. Hedging will use short sales, derivative contracts, or a combination of the two. Hedging may not always be direct; for instance, a long position in IBM shares may not necessarily be hedged by a short position in IBM shares. It may be more economical to short-sell shares in another security that shares many of the same characteristics. The key to this strategy is that this share must have greater downside potential and cost less to borrow. An example of such a hedge could be the sale of one S&P futures contract for every 2500 IBM shares held (the amount determined by the relative sensitivity of the two securities and their monetary denominations). Another hedge could involve the short sale in Japan of 100 shares of NEC (Nippon Electric Co., a Japanese computer manufacturer) for every IBM share held (the amounts determined once again by the relative sensitivity of the two securities and their monetary denominations).

- *Arbitrage.*   This strategy involves attempts to exploit temporary price inefficiencies or discrepancies between securities or markets. These strategies are rarely true risk-free arbitrages [i.e., exploiting price differences between fully fungible assets]. In today's markets, these arbitrages typically rely on historical relationships between instruments in different markets to identify and exploit aberrations from "historical" patterns. This is generally an area in which many hedge fund "misadventures" occur, given the misleading data series and the heroic assumptions often used to identify the "historical." Given the ever-increasing efficiency of the financial markets, the returns on many of these investments are minuscule; thus the only way a fund can enhance such returns is by assembling large positions through leverage (see the following paragraph).

- *Leveraging.*   This strategy involves either borrowing money, to increase the effective size of the portfolio; or assigning cash or securities as down payment, collateral, or margin for a percentage of the position one seeks to establish.

- *Synthetic positions or derivatives.*   This strategy involves using derivative contracts to establish positions or strategies. These contracts often simplify the creation of an investment position (e.g., a short sale) by having a bank or financial intermediary deal with the mechanics of establishing positions and then simply assuming from them the potential upside and/or downside associated with the underlying position held by the bank.

As we can see from this list, alternative investment vehicles cover a broad spectrum of activities and operations, many of which have little in common with one another.

Hedge Fund Diversity versus Commonality

Is there really such a thing as a representative hedge fund? It is common to speak of hedge funds as single, easily recognized entities. However, the term *hedge fund* has no legal definition and is in fact misleading. As we saw in the preceding list, many alternative investment programs may not regularly employ hedging techniques to generate their returns. Furthermore, given the variety of techniques and markets in which they operate, there really is no such thing as an archetypal hedge fund on which to hang a generalization.

Investment history can, however, give us some insight into what modern hedge funds do have in common. Many of the methods used by today's hedge funds trace their parentage to those used by the investment syndicates and trusts of the 1920s. These syndicates gained considerable notoriety in the markets of the time by taking speculative, often destabilizing, long and short positions in stocks, bonds, and commodities with the objective of maximizing their investors' returns. However, despite superficial similarities, modern hedge funds are different, given the sophistication of their operations and the markets in which they operate. Today's markets do not easily tolerate the outright market manipulations and financial skullduggery that were the hallmark of these vehicles in the 1920s. It is, therefore, safer to proclaim an investment partnership formed in 1949 by Alfred Winslow Jones, a U.S.-based Australian, as the first true hedge fund. The goal of his fund was to generate profits through superior stock picking, using two of the speculative techniques described in the preceding list: short selling to protect a portion of his portfolio against adverse market movements and leverage to magnify his portfolio's returns. He also designed a merit-based compensation arrangement in which he was paid a percentage of the profits generated from his clients' assets, the forerunner of the profit-sharing fees so common in hedge funds today. Despite an excellent track record and all the trappings of a modern hedge fund, this partnership operated in relative anonymity for nearly 10 years.

A. W. Jones's fund was a maverick for its time because it emphasized manager skills to generate its returns. Traditional investments in stocks and bonds undertaken by collective investment vehicles such as mutual funds are generally of the buy-and-hold variety with little or no leverage. This means they rely for the most part on movement of the underlying markets to generate their returns. On the other hand, alternative vehicles and investment programs rely heavily on, and reward handsomely, the skill of managers, who are generally given a wider investment brief than their mutual fund counterparts. David White, a former chief investment officer at the

Rockefeller Foundation, argues that an estimated 80 percent of the returns generated by traditional managers come from the market and 20 percent from skill. With alternative investments, he claims that the ratio is reversed.

Thus, this heavy reliance on manager skills is the common denominator of hedge funds. Perhaps the best way to define alternative investments would be to call them "skill-based strategies."

For the purposes of this book we define a *hedge fund* as any investment vehicle that uses a combination of some or all of the investment techniques outlined in the preceding list, and whose manager receives an incentive fee on the outcome of these strategies. This is admittedly a broad definition, but in light of the diversity of the hedge fund universe, it is the most practical.

CHAPTER 2

Some Trends and Fallacies Regarding Hedge Funds

HEDGE FUND MANAGERS TODAY

In the nearly 50 years (at the time of writing) since the birth of A. W. Jones's hedge fund, the financial industry has seen a proliferation of new financial instruments, markets, and trading opportunities, which go well beyond those envisioned in the A. W. Jones partnership.

Today, under the designation of *hedge fund*, we find a heterogeneous collection of investment vehicles, operating amid a mind-boggling array of markets, using a wide variety of investment techniques.

To make sense of this bewildering universe, it is common to classify hedge funds in terms of what they invest in or do. Following this criterion it is possible to find some 32 different types of hedge funds in today's alternative investment universe. A short but by no means exhaustive list of these fund types is as follows:

- Macro funds
- Special-situation funds
- Pure equity funds
- Convertible arbitrage funds
- Funds of funds

- Market-neutral funds
- Commodity trading advisor funds
- Private equity funds
- Risk arbitrage funds
- Long or short funds
- Emerging market funds
- Marco funds
- Event risk funds
- Restructured or defaulted security funds

Such a classification is useful to give the reader some idea of the richness and variety of hedge funds in existence. It is, however, of little practical use in analyzing the viability or advisability of an investment in hedge funds, aside from alerting us to the problems of using one tool to evaluate them all. Other attempts to analyze and classify hedge funds rely on other criteria such as

- Asset class utilized
- Investment strategy utilized
- Market exposure
- Geographic concentration
- Level of diversification
- Hedged or unhedged
- Portfolio turnover or liquidity
- Use of leverage

Such classifications yield us little in terms of analytical insight, and these criteria can be misleading. As competition among alternative investments increases, many funds are constantly seeking to increase their returns, diversify their risks, and attract new investors. This often means that managers, aided by broad investment mandates outlined in their prospectuses, are constantly branching out into new fields or incorporating new or different activities in their operations. This ongoing metamorphosis among so many funds dulls the usefulness of descriptive classifications such as the ones outlined above. Often these labels have caused unwary investors to draw incorrect conclusions about the type of investment they were making.

It is more productive to stop and look at why investing in hedge funds can be interesting for an investor, and to see if we can't find a more powerful tool to analyze hedge funds from these factors.

CLASSIFYING HEDGE FUNDS USING THE VALUE-ADDED FACTOR

Modern portfolio theory has taught us that through a careful combination of financial assets it is possible to create an investment portfolio that provides investors with superior returns and lower volatility (risk) than any of the separate components of the portfolio could have done alone. In this context, adding hedge funds to a portfolio makes sense only when they can increase the returns of our portfolio while decreasing its overall volatility.

In reviewing hedge funds, savvy investors are not really interested in the absolute returns generated by a manager or in the manager's fund's absolute risk. What they are really looking for are hedge funds that can generate incremental portfolio returns for less than proportional increments in portfolio risk. We shall identify this characteristic as the manager's value-added factor. In order to evaluate hedge funds effectively, we want to identify the tradeoff between incremental portfolio risks and returns a hedge fund manager adds to our portfolio.

Traditionally it has been argued that hedge funds do generate such benefits consistently. However, before going on to show how much of this rests on common fallacies and misconceptions, we need to understand how the value-added factor can be used to classify hedge funds.

Classification-based tools fall short of providing investors insight into what a portfolio can do for them. Rather, an alternative is to rank and evaluate funds in terms of the value-added that a specific fund could bring to an investor's portfolio. A handy way of doing this is to use a two-step process:

(1) assessing a given fund's overall exposure to broad market movements and (2) evaluating the effect of this exposure on the fund's risk/return characteristics. In general, through this process we find that the higher a fund's degree of *directionality*, or investing in market direction, the higher the fund's potential return and volatility will be. This, in turn, will influence the risk/return characteristics that the fund will bring when added to an investor's portfolio. Using such an approach, we can identify three broad hedge fund categories: (1) relative value, (2) value/net long bias, and (3) market-directional.

In *relative-value* hedge funds, annual target rates of return are usually around 10 percent gross of fees. These funds emphasize risk avoidance and seek to generate consistent, moderate returns with low volatility. This category includes managers using so-called market-neutral or nondirectional strategies (in practice, however, these strategies are often anything but market-neutral or nondirectional). These can include long/short investing (in equal amounts), options, and futures trading, as well as the following strategies:

- Equity arbitrage
- Fixed-income arbitrage
- Risk or special-event arbitrage

In hedge funds in the *value/net long bias* category, annual target rates of return are usually some multiple of the return on the stock market index, generally the S&P 500. These funds emphasize a moderate amount of exposure to the market, as well as some directional investing. Typically, a portion of the portfolio will be hedged, while the other portion is not. The original A. W. Jones program would fall into this category. Strategies included in this category include the *traditional hedged long/short portfolio,* specifically one that purchases under-valued securities and sells short overvalued ones.

In *pure-market-directional* hedge funds, annual target rates of return are usually around 20 to 30 percent gross of fees but are highly volatile and unpredictable. These funds emphasize more aggressive plays and seek high returns. This type of fund will, for example, place large leveraged bets on a small number of anticipated events. If these bets are correct, managers can generate profits in many different market environments. In this category we find *global/macro* funds, which seek to exploit opportunistic investment possibilities wherever they may be found; and *trend-following futures funds,* which seek to capture the movements and capitalize on the leverage in the futures, commodities, and currency markets.

As we can see from Table 2.1, these categories, based on the sensitivity to market exposure that we suggested above, seem to correspond neatly to the characteristics of major hedge fund groupings where higher returns and volatility are generally associated with greater reliance on market directionality.

TABLE 2.1

Hedge Fund Annual Returns and Annual Standard Deviation, January 1994 to December 1998

Fund Type	Average Annual Returns (%)	Average Annual Standard Deviation (%)
Relative value		
Market-neutral	10.678	0.38824026
Relative value	10.26	0.51720337
Merger	12.652	0.52156633
Convertible arbitrage	9.77	0.53130367
Value/net long bias		
Mortgage	9.838	0.68061263
Distressed	10.344	0.77347238
Market timing	12.856	0.81382689
Event-driven	14.592	0.87983866
Market-directional		
Equity hedge	16.114	1.08259954
Macro	11.098	1.10107974
Emerging market	2.256	2.10224364

Source: Lara Capital and Hfr.

Having understood that it is possible to categorize hedge funds and what some of the characteristics associated with some of the major hedge fund types are, let's now stop and look at some of the common fallacies associated with hedge funds.

SOME COMMON FALLACIES REGARDING HEDGE FUNDS

Defining a hedge fund as a "skill-based investment" is a very useful tool. On the other hand, one should treat with a certain amount of skepticism the claim that since alternative investments rely on the manager's skills for over 80 percent of their returns, they can generate superior returns "in all conditions and environments." We shall quickly review some fallacies that arise from this line of thought.

Hedge Funds Generate Strong Returns in All Market Conditions

The fallacy of this can quickly be seen from Table 2.1, which shows that emerging market hedge funds returned only 2.3 percent average annual return in over 4 years. Their performance, as is testified by the high standard deviation number, was heavily influenced by events in emerging markets at the end of 1998. As mentioned, certain types of funds use a wide degree of market sensitivity to generate their returns. The greater this sensitivity in difficult market conditions, the greater their chance of losses.

Hedge Funds Can Reduce Exposure to the U.S. Stock Market

This belief is based on the fact that many hedge funds do not depend on the U.S. stock market, or more generally its proxy, the S&P 500 index, to generate their returns. However, this belief is wrong for two reasons. It ignores both the S&P's tidal effect on all financial markets, domestic and worldwide, and the limited history on which this claim is based.

It is important to remember that few hedge funds existed before 1980, and the majority have been formed in the early- to mid-1990s, an exceptionally favorable environment for investment activities. Some heart-stopping financial volatility occurred during this time, especially in October 1987, September 1994, and August 1998, but these were limited events whose duration rarely lasted more than a few months. At no point since the late 1980s have we seen or experienced a period of sustained and consistent adverse conditions in the financial markets. We believe it is safe to say that a sustained bear market has not tested the majority of managers. It remains to be seen whether hedge funds as a whole will be able to deliver consistent performance in difficult markets, and so these observations should be approached with a fair degree of skepticism.

Furthermore, in a period of rising financial assets it is inevitable that the returns of even the most adept, skill-based managers will be influenced by the favorable climate in financial assets. The dramatic rise in the U.S. stock market from 1980 to 1998 as shown in Chart 2.1 undoubtedly had an important effect (either direct or indirect) on alternative investment managers.

A hint of the S&P's influence on hedge fund performance can be gleaned by looking at Chart 2.2, which shows the distribution of monthly returns of a composite hedge fund index in excess of the S&P 500 stock market index over an 18-year period. In other words, looking at hedge funds as a whole, Chart 2.2 shows the frequency with which monthly hedge fund returns have tracked those of the U.S. stock market. Chart 2.2 shows that most hedge fund returns are closely tied to the value of the S&P 500. From January 1994 to December 1998, approximately 43 percent of the hedge fund returns

CHART 2.1

The S&P 500 index from November 1980 to December 1998.

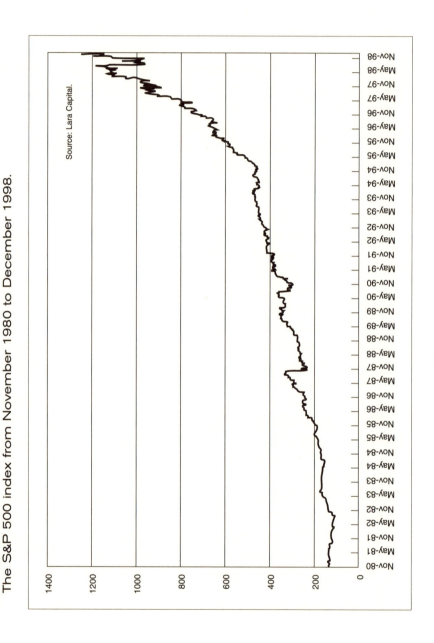

Source: Lara Capital.

14

were within ±1 percent, and over 60 percent were within ±2 percent of the S&P[1] returns. This kind of concentration tells us nothing about the cause of this concentration nor whether this phenomenon will repeat itself in the future and in down markets. Nonetheless, readers should question the accepted doctrine with a little more diligence.

Hedge Funds Are "Safer" than Traditional Asset Classes or Managers

Traditional fund managers have investment mandates that typically constrain them to hold assets in a well-defined number of asset classes and are frequently limited to little or no leverage. Hedge fund managers, on the other hand, typically have mandates that give them the flexibility to choose among many asset classes and to employ dynamic trading strategies that frequently involve short sales, leverage, and derivatives. Because traditional managers are essentially limited to buy-and-hold strategies, their returns are highly correlated (i.e., their returns are similar to, or track those) to traditional asset classes such as stocks, bonds, and commodities.

Because of their greater investment flexibility, hedge funds are generally touted as superior investments. This flexibility gives them the ability to generate returns that have a low or negative correlation to mutual funds and standard asset classes. In other words, it is claimed that because hedge fund returns do not track those of other asset classes, they are safer. However, investors should bear in mind an important distinction. Correlation and exposure are two very different concepts. It is well publicized that many hedge funds use the same liquid asset classes that traditional managers use. For example, George Soros's Quantum Fund was long U.S. stocks and short Japanese stocks during the October 1987 stock market crash.

---

1. Because of its construction, this index gives equal weighting to equity-based hedge managers and has a slight stock market bias. However, over the time period considered this bias is relatively negligible.

CHART 2.2

Monthly hedge fund returns in excess of the S&P 500 index from November 1980 to December 1998.

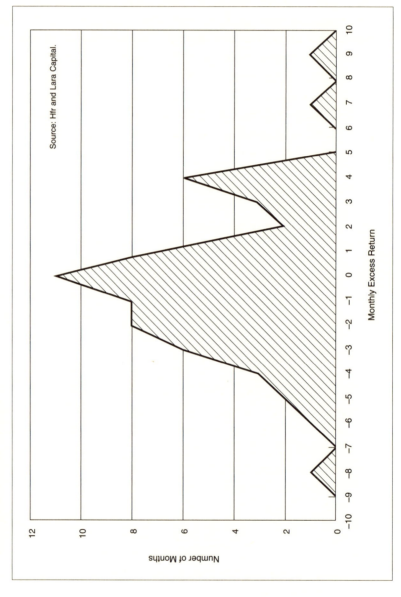

Source: Hfr and Lara Capital.

He was then short the British pound in September 1992, long precious metals in April 1993, and long the U.S. dollar but short the Japanese yen in February 1994. Yet Quantum's returns appear to have low correlations to these asset classes, both overall and during those periods. Clearly, the constantly changing selection of investments and level of leverage of the Quantum Fund must have had a great influence on this fund's performance and thus its correlation with other asset classes.

To illustrate this point, consider a manager who trades S&P futures contracts. Without leverage, a fully invested position of being consistently long one futures contract (i.e., buy-and-hold position) means that the manager will have a correlation coefficient of 1 to the S&P 500 index. Conversely, if this manager is short one futures contract, the correlation coefficient will be -1. However, if the manager alternates between long and short each month, the regression coefficient will be close to zero, as the long market–short market correlation averages out. The manager, however, is operating in and is subject to the risks of the S&P market, i.e., being short a rising S&P and vice versa.

This means that while a hedge fund may have a low correlation to an asset class, its risk book, or the amount and size of the risks it has open, can be heavily biased toward that asset. In other words, low correlation to a market or asset and no exposure to that market are not the same thing. Investors should bear in mind that if they take the low correlation of a hedge fund to an asset class without a careful analysis, they could find an unpleasant surprise in their portfolio in the future.

Conclusion

This analysis of common hedge fund fallacies highlights the danger of constructing hedge fund investment portfolios. Without careful analysis and an understanding of what they are doing, investors could find themselves at greater risk than they had anticipated. This is particularly true for investors who are seeking to reduce their exposure to certain asset classes via hedge funds, or increase the returns on a traditional asset portfolio, and are looking for hedge funds to introduce uncorrelated returns to their portfolios.

This doesn't mean that hedge funds can't provide yield enhancement and diversification to an investor's portfolio—just that in order to do so, it is necessary to look at things from a slightly different perspective, and do lots and lots of homework. This requires obtaining and analyzing hedge fund information.

CHAPTER 3

Hedge Fund Analysis

ANALYZING HEDGE FUNDS: THE IMPORTANCE OF INFORMATION

How and where does one obtain information to analyze and categorize hedge funds? The fund's prospectus is generally a good starting point. This document should contain information on the hedge fund's stated investment strategy and philosophy, as well as its track record. This information should give us a rough idea as to which of the three groups (relative value, value/net long, or directional) the fund might belong. However, hedge fund prospectuses are often written in the more obscure dialects of legalese. They may also be so generic as to be of little practical use. Furthermore, managers often alter their investment strategies to suit market circumstances and their own particular needs. It is important to also spend some time looking at and analyzing a manager's track record. The question is where one obtains the data needed to perform these evaluations.

Until recently, investing in hedge funds was difficult and tricky because their operations were surrounded in mystique and secrecy. Their opportunities were accessible exclusively to the superaffluent and the well informed. There are many reasons for the myth of secrecy. Some are cultural; many hedge fund managers are graduates of the proprietary desks of investment banks where secrecy is the paramount rule. Some reasons are practical; many managers are reluctant to disclose excessive information on their positions for fear that this information could be exploited at their expense by other market participants ("busting" their short positions, etc.).

Many hedge funds also seem to surround themselves in secrecy and mystique to increase their appeal to investors. The press has recently done much to exaggerate the aspects of risk, wealth, and mystery surrounding hedge funds and their investments and operations. One should never underestimate the brief *frisson* which, thanks to the press, hedge fund investing can generate in the minds of investors. Nor should one underestimate the ability of hedge fund marketers to capitalize on this. This brings us to the last, and often most important, reason for perceived limitation on hedge fund information.

Ironically, for an industry dedicated to allegedly exploiting inefficiencies in the financial markets, the hedge fund market itself is (in financial terms) an imperfect market. Its operation is heavily dependent on a whole host of intermediaries devoted to matching buyers (investors) and sellers (investment managers), who have every reason to limit the flow of information to the public. The existence of these agents owes much to the way the industry is structured. Most hedge funds tend to be minimally staffed, entrepreneurial organizations, often little known even in their own fields. Conversely, many investors have limited resources at their disposal. They either have time limitations, seek anonymity, or both if they are private individuals. Investors who operate as institutions or corporations need outside experts to perform or confirm their in-house searches and evaluations. These intermediaries, who match buyers with sellers and do searches and verifications, obtain substantial commissions for their efforts (often from both the buyers and the sellers, their impartiality skewed by the best bidder), are anxious to maintain a lack of transparency in this market to protect their role.

This means that while managers may be willing to provide information to investors, the agents have a vested interest in limiting the distribution of this information, for fear of losing their commission stream.

However, things are beginning to change. Falling interest rates, decreasing brokerage commissions, and the desire for double-digit returns by the investing public have propelled the growth of alternative investments since the mid-1990s. Furthermore, as traditional managers seek to enhance both their performance and their pay, many of the techniques and operating characteristics of hedge funds (leverage, use of derivative contracts, incentive fees, etc.) are slowly passing into the mainstream investing world. The numerous restrictions placed on such activities by regulators in local markets are slowly being loosened to conform to offshore practices, and are accelerating this process.

As competition for the investor's dollar increases, hedge funds—true to their flexibility and with a well-tuned ear to the demands of their potential investors and international regulators—have been increasing their transparency. A growing number of publications and sources now offer hedge fund information and data, loosening the hold of intermediaries on this market. Laws are also changing to allow wider dissemination of hedge fund performance and manager information. In a landmark decision, the U.S. Securities and Exchange Commission ruled in 1997 that hedge funds could distribute data using an Internet subscriber service, provided only "qualified investors" have access to this information. This is clearly the beginning of a trend that will soon allow investors, already mesmerized by the power of online brokerage, to run data-alternative investment searches, track their investment's net asset value (NAV), and download performance histories and fund prospectuses.

While gathering data becomes easier than ever, evaluating fund performance and identifying products that best meet investors' requirements becomes more complex.

ANALYZING HEDGE FUNDS: SEEKING TRUTH FROM THE FACTS

All good, consistent financial decisions are an art rather than a science. With information on alternative investments still far from perfect, successful hedge fund investing is truly a black art which requires insight, research, and attention to detail.

There are two key strands to selecting alternative investment managers: the *quantitative,* the analysis of managers' numbers; and the *qualitative,* the analysis of managers themselves and the markets in which they operate. One cannot overemphasize the importance of qualitative analysis and manager due diligence. A sound due-diligence process is part detective work, part psychology, and part keen industry insight.

Many funds, especially those offered by successful marketers, come in slick presentation packages with attractive track records and reams of quantitative information to back up the claims that the investment vehicle they are representing is the "Next Great Thing."

Needless to say, such presentations should be taken with a healthy degree of skepticism. The two phrases "past performance is no indication of future results" and "lies, damn lies, and statistics" should always be in the back of investors' minds.

A track record of monthly returns tells only a fraction of a manager's story; however, the data it provides investors can be used to develop tests to:

- Screen managers who show high probabilities of continuing to deliver results and determine the impact of random factors (luck, market trends, etc.) on a manager's performance

- Detect misinformation (misrepresentation of results, style drift)
- Generate red flags requiring further investigation or due diligence

These are not minor issues. The history of hedge funds is already littered with a few spectacularly notable failures, which could have been identified if investors had been looking in the right places and had performed thorough due diligence.

ANALYZING HEDGE FUNDS: THE PROBLEMS WITH TRACK RECORDS

Aside from the prospectus, a key source of hedge fund information is a fund's track record. In analyzing a manager's track record, investors should always keep in mind that past performance is no indication of future results. The story that past performance tells is in the past, per se; it tells us nothing about what the manager can or will do in the future. But what exactly is a track record?

The purchase or sale of hedge fund shares is determined by the value of the underlying assets. These are calculated by taking the value of the fund's cash, plus open positions, less its debt. This method of measuring a fund value is called the *net asset value* (NAV). An investor's return from a hedge fund investment is thus given by the changes in the value of his hedge fund shares, or the NAV of the fund.[1] A hedge fund track record is simply the historical presentation of the fund's historical returns as measured by the changes in its value over time. A track record will tell us how a fund's NAV has changed over time. However, before using track records to make hedge fund valuations, we need to be aware of a few caveats.

---

1. Assuming that the fund has paid no dividends or made any capital distributions to investors.

Historical Returns: The Relevance Problem

Many funds present *pro forma returns*—theoretical returns of what the fund could have made in the past had such a methodology, manager, or asset composition been used. Pro forma statements are particularly common with

- Funds of funds, where the track records of existing managers are combined according to some weighting determined by the fund promoter, generally with 20/20 hindsight
- New hedge funds, where managers rely on previous track records at investment banks or funds to illustrate their investment skills
- System-following commodity trading advisers (CTAs) interested in showing how their system would have performed in the past, had it been used

Since they have not been validated by actual market events, pro forma track records should not be considered as relevant in evaluating managers and should be questioned accordingly.

Historical Returns: The Consistency Problem

Conventional wisdom says that the longer we have returns for a manager, the better and more precise our evaluation of this manager will be. Actually, this is a dubious assertion. Financial markets are constantly changing, at times with frightening speed. When looking at track records longer than 5 years, unless we have proof to the contrary, we should always assume that the techniques and investments used by the manager might have changed. This is not necessarily unfavorable; a manager who can successfully adapt to changing markets and continue to perform is to be sought after. However, changing investments and techniques render comparisons between and across years difficult and misleading, since we may not be comparing apples to apples.

Chart 3.1 shows the real 10-year track record of the Clever Fund.[2] The numbers have been massaged to highlight how the variation of monthly returns (as measured by standard deviation) changed, as the manager moved away from managing money personally (years 1 to 3), to investing money with other managers (years 4 to 10). Thanks to this shift, it is clear that we are not looking at the same type of investment program. The fund's reduced risk is not due to the manager's performance per se. Rather, it depends on those of the other managers whose performance is not detailed in the prospectus. Any attempt to analyze 10 years of the Clever Fund data without adjusting for the radical change in strategy will result in a substantially flawed analysis.

Historical Returns: Fees

We should always check to see that all management, performance, and administration fees have been deducted from our performance numbers. We should also check the prospectus, to see if there are additional fees associated with share purchases and redemption, and then adjust track record data to reflect this. Given the wide array and diversity of fees, both explicit and hidden, it is important when comparing funds to ensure that track record return numbers are from net of fees. This ensures that the data are consistent and thus meaningful for comparison.

Historical Returns: Valuations

We saw that a NAV requires that the assets and liabilities of a fund be valued at a prevailing market price. There are different techniques for doing this:

- *Marked to spot.*   The prevailing spot price for the asset is used. This works fine for one-dimensional assets such

---

2. The fund name has been changed at the manager's request.

CHART 3.1

The Clever Fund, showing 10-year changes in monthly standard deviation.

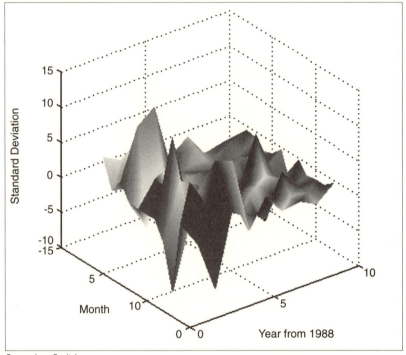

Source: Lara Capital.

as stocks, where the market price is truly their replacement price. For assets with more than one dimension, such as derivative contracts, the market price is seldom their replacement price, because of the impact of other factors such as time value and volatility, which can have a substantial impact on the asset's replacement price. The marked-to-spot technique is an inaccurate measure of the value of a fund's positions and assets. It gives us no assurance that the price used to compute the NAV is the price at which we could liquidate the portfolio in the market.

- *Marked to model.*   The theoretical price of the asset is determined by using a mathematical model which captures the spot price and the other dimensions of an asset's value such as time value and volatility, which determine the asset's value. The problem with this approach is that in many circumstances the market prices for a financial asset can be very different from the computer-generated theoretical price. Once again, the model price gives us no assurance that computing a portfolio NAV using this price is the actual price at which we could liquidate the assets in the market.

- *Marked to market.*   The prevailing market price is used for the asset, whose value is measured at the true replacement price. This is clearly the best and the most effective method for valuing a fund. An investor should always seek to clarify how the market price is determined. As long as the assets are liquid, finding accurate market prices is relatively straightforward. The issue becomes tricky when the assets of the fund are less liquid. In such cases the investment manager may personally furnish the price to the administrator, or the price may come from broker-dealers, who may have a vested interest in providing a manager with attractive prices. In other cases managers may participate so prominently in a relatively nonliquid market that they can influence the prices to suit their own needs. These latter cases should be taken under advisement, as they can provide managers with scope to misreport a fund's true value and boost their own performance (and thus fees), or hide losses. This is a story that unfortunately appears with disturbing regularity. Investors should always keep their ears tuned for the possibility of such occurrences.

Clearly, all these factors will have a large impact on the validity of a track record for analytical purposes. Most of these issues need to be addressed in detail at the moment of due diligence, and investors who skip asking such detailed questions do so at their peril.

Historical Returns: The Ax Problem

Unless verified in the due-diligence process, long track records may also hide other issues that make meaningful evaluation difficult. These issues include changes in managers, strategy, leverage, and markets.

All these issues can lead the unwary investor into the ax paradox. The paradox poses the following question: If I have an ax, and after 3 years I change the handle, and after 2 more years I change the blade, do I still have the same ax at the end of 5 years? In other words, in reviewing a long track record, we should not focus on the length of the track record per se, but only on the portions of it which are relevant to the manager's present activities.

Historical Returns: The Moving-Target Problem

Alternative investments are extremely flexible vehicles, capable of changing their exposure or risk books in a day, should the need arise. Given this flexibility, we should be aware that most hedge fund NAVs give us only a summary of the fund's activities. Since they are static numbers, they tell us little about the value of the fund and how its investments have changed.

To understand this issue better, let us return to the example of the George Soros Quantum Fund during September 1992. Market lore has it that during that period Quantum made in excess of U.S. $1.8 billion by shorting sterling against the deutsche mark.

Chart 3.2 looks at the changes in the sterling–deutsche mark cross (exchange) rate and changes in the value of the Quantum Fund from July to December 1992. Given the size of the sterling devaluation, and Quantum's reported profit, quick

CHART 3.2

Sterling-deutsche mark cross (exchange) rate (labeled "stg/dem cross" in diagram) versus Quantum Fund changes in value from July 1, 1992 to December 31, 1992 (July 1, 1992 = 100 percent).

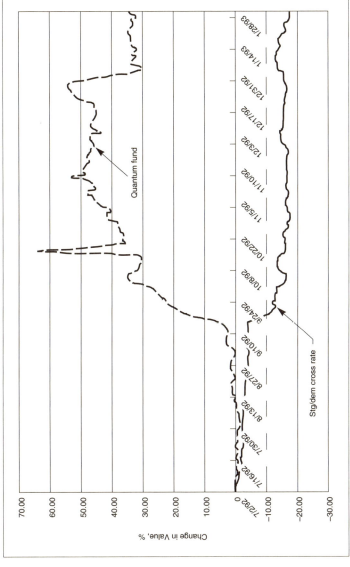

Source: Lara Capital.

29

back-of-the envelope calculations reveal that the fund's sterling position must have been around U.S. $10 billion, or roughly twice the fund's stated capital during that period. Because of the size of the position and its payoff, we would expect Quantum's returns during that period to be closely correlated to the sterling–deutsche mark cross rate. As we can see from Chart 3.2, the movements in Quantum's daily NAV and the cross rate seem to track one another for only a very short period. This is confirmed by looking at the correlation coefficient of the Quantum Fund's returns to sterling during the period. It turns out that it is 0.23 for monthly return data, while using daily data, it is less than 0.10. Why is this? Chart 3.2 shows that the bulk of the position must have been put on September 11, and taken off September 22. This means that the position was put on and taken off during the month.

Since the bulk of the sterling position was opened and closed within the month of September, other factors will also have influenced Quantum's returns, and unless we have that information, what little we have been able to infer about the fund and its activities are meaningless.

In other words, if we do not know exactly what a fund's positions are in real time, reviewing and evaluating even daily fund valuations will tell us little or nothing about what risks the fund is taking to generate its results. Thus, the more a fund is market-directional, the more it trades, and the more it trades, the greater the chance that it may change positions and leverage in a short time. In such cases, only with perfect and full disclosure of a manager's positions in real time can performance numbers tell us what a fund is really up to.

Conclusion

With all these caveats in mind, it becomes clear that a hedge fund track record should be treated and looked at differently from that of a mutual fund.

With a mutual fund, the underlying buy-and-hold track record ensures that the returns of the fund will track the asset in which it invests very closely. It is therefore relatively straightforward to compare a manager's performance to that of the underlying asset to determine the manager's ability. Because of the constraint imposed by the buy-and-hold strategy, manager skill will contribute only about 20 percent to a fund's overall return. With hedge funds this is not the case. For this reason hedge fund track records give us very little insight into the nature and type of the underlying investments. Nor can they be used to determine a fund's exposure to specific asset classes or market movements. Furthermore, the lack of correlation of a hedge fund's track record to a specific asset class give us no assurance about being insulated from movements in that asset class. In fact, the only thing a track record can tell us is how a manager has behaved. To interpret this in a meaningful manner, we need to extract from a track record the amount of risk a manager undertook in generating results.

CHAPTER 4

Financial Risk and Hedge Funds

RISK: A GENERAL DEFINITION

Extracting meaningful information from a fund track record requires trying to identify how much risk a manager took to generate results. This, in turn, requires developing an understanding of risk.

In our daily lives we tend to look at risk as something dangerous—something to be avoided if we want a long, calm, and happy life. In actuality, risk is a probabilistic event. The *American Heritage Dictionary* defines risk as "the possibility of suffering harm, loss, or danger. A factor or course involving uncertain danger." Put into plain English this means that falling off a 1000-ft cliff will kill me, but it is not risky if I happen to be miles from the nearest cliff. Only if I am in a situation where I may actually fall off a 1000-ft cliff, does falling off a cliff become a risky event for me. So risk is not the outcome of a harmful event, just the chance (or probability) that it might occur.

Risk in the financial markets is also determined by uncertainty—specifically, the uncertainty associated with the outcome of an investment, position, investment manager, or fund we undertake.

FINANCIAL RISK: DISTINGUISHING CHARACTERISTICS

In many ways financial risk is structurally different from the risk we encounter in our everyday lives. This is because financial risk always has a reward attached for those who accept it and conversely entails a cost for those who seek to avoid it.

Since their birth in the Italian renaissance, uncertainty and its remuneration have been an integral and vital part of the financial markets. Today more than ever the workings of the global financial markets depend on their ability to reward investors for the risks they take and charge them for risks they seek to avoid. If anything, this process has become more efficient. Since the early 1980s, vast resources and ingenuity have been poured into successfully identifying and unbundling many of the different types of risks (currency, interest rate, commodity, equity, credit, etc.) present in financial markets. Thanks to this process, today's investors can regulate their financial activities with great sophistication: pricing and comparing the types of risk they are willing to accept, analyzing and costing those they decline. This allows them to tailor their portfolio returns and risks with great precision.

But why are risk and remuneration so closely connected in the financial markets? In principle, the answer is easy. Nobody will willingly undertake a risky investment (an investment whose final outcome is unknown) without receiving some kind of reward greater than the risk undertaken. Investors will buy bonds sold by certain companies only if they feel the bonds' coupons are sufficient to compensate them for the possibility that the company in question may default before the bond matures. Thus, given the probability of an unfavorable investment outcome, effective investors will always seek a level of remuneration that will, over time, compensate them for the losses they will face when the unfavorable event materializes.

When the unfavorable event occurs, an investor who was insufficiently remunerated for the risk will face a net loss. An investor who does this sort of thing consistently will lose all investment capital and be forced to leave the investment scene. On the other hand, if an investor obtains excessive remuneration for the actual risks personally borne, other investors will soon want in. This competition will eventually bring the level of remuneration back to a level accurately reflecting the actual probability of the risk's occurrence. Through these mechanisms financial markets have a neat and effective way to balance risk and reward, ensuring that it is always correctly priced, at least in theory. Real-world financial markets are far more complex.

FINANCIAL RISK: ITS COMPLEX AND DYNAMIC NATURE

In the preceding section we saw that the very essence of financial markets is the constant interplay between risk and rewards, the perception of the future and its actual outcome. In modern financial markets stocks, bonds, commodities, and currencies are constantly changing in value, in some cases by the second. This means that financial risk and reward are changing all the time, often substantially during the course of a day. To complicate matters further, not only is financial risk dynamic; it is determined by a large set of factors, some knowable and predictable and some unknowable and random. This means that risk is too complex to be measured in a meaningful way with any degree of accuracy. With this limitation in mind, the best an investor can hope to do is to estimate it. This will require investors to use historical data and statistical tools, hoping that what happened in the past will continue to hold in the future, hoping that their calculations are correct, and hoping that they have not ignored some minor but crucial detail. This considerably complicates the interplay between risk and reward, although over time the basic principles outlined in the preceding section will hold.

Because investors cannot measure an investment's exact risk and reward, they must rely on their estimation that it is so.

This, in turn, is based on a series of educated guesses using statistical tools of differing degrees of sophistication. Guesses are by definition inaccurate and flawed. Investors are always exposed to the constant dynamic interplay between the perceived and actual outcome of a risk event. In doing so, investors are forced to rely on the perception that an investment's remuneration is fair on the basis of their own determination of the risks. There is no assurance that the perceived remuneration will be the exact remuneration for the actual risk borne by the investor.

With this in mind, we begin to understand how risk and reward in today's financial markets may be very much in the eyes of the beholder. The same financial asset can be bought and sold by investors with different risk and loss thresholds. Each investor is driven by a subjective perception of the asset's risk/reward tradeoff. Despite these subjective interpretations of risk, reality will always intrude to keep things more or less in balance. No investor can consistently misjudge risk for long periods of time. Differences between an event's perceived risk and its occurrence will be eventually corrected. Investors who underestimated the correct level of remuneration for the risk's occurrence will be penalized by larger-than-expected losses on their investments.

From this cursory description we can see how many of the arbitrages (statistical, convergence, relative value, etc.) popular with many different types of hedge fund managers can contain greater risk than what is readily apparent. Any flaw in the assumptions or the data underlying the arbitrage can, in fact, cause a divergence between the arbitrage's actual and perceived risk. This inevitably leads to unpleasant surprises when the actual risks turn out to have been greater than the perceived risks, and the remuneration received woefully inadequate for the loss suffered.

The constant, dynamic interplay between actual risk and its subjective evaluation is the spice of investing. Consistently estimating risk correctly is the black art of investing and the stuff of legendary investors and superior hedge fund performance. Unfortunately, misjudging risk is the single largest cause of investment losses, financial collapses, and other misadventures that befall hedge fund investors.

RISK: IDENTIFYING IT IN HEDGE FUNDS

If I invest in a hedge fund, I want to know what will happen to my investment. After some time has gone by, is it going to be greater, smaller, or the same as my initial investment?

The traditional technique used to assess this uncertainty has been to use the potential variability of an investment's expected returns as a proxy for a fund's riskiness. Intuitively, the approach makes sense. If we are seeking managers with strong investment skills, we are looking to identify funds or managers that give us strong, consistent investment performance. The riskier the investment, the wider the range of potential outcomes associated with its returns. In other words, a "safe" investment is one whose outcome is "predictable" because the manager's track record has shown little variation over time. To understand this better, let us look at the actual hedge fund track records of a low- and a high-risk fund.[1]

The Steady Fund illustrated in Chart 4.1 is a classic example of a "low"-risk fund as it generated average returns of 0.5 percent every month over a $6^1/_2$ year period, with few surprises.

On the other hand, the Marsh Fund, illustrated in Chart 4.2, is an example of a "high"-risk fund, as its track record shows a greater variability of monthly returns over the same $6^1/_2$-year period.

Comparison of Charts 4.1 and 4.2 reveals that the Marsh Fund's returns have a greater range of fluctuation than do those of the Steady Fund. Because of this volatility, the Marsh Fund's returns are harder to predict with any degree of confidence. It is

---

[1] Fund names were changed at the manager's request.

CHART 4.1

Steady Fund monthly returns from January 1990 to June 1996.

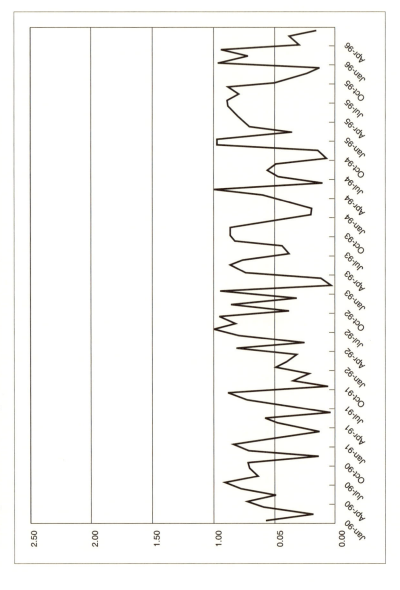

Source: Lara Capital.

CHART 4.2

Marsh Fund monthly returns from January 1990 to June 1996.

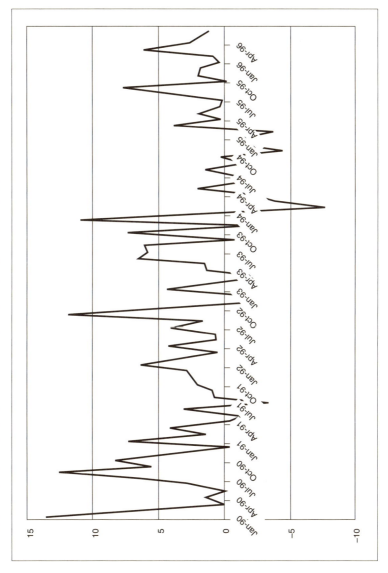

Source: Lara Capital.

for this reason that an investment in the Marsh Fund would be traditionally considered riskier.

Capitalizing on the insight that financial risk is the variability of outcomes, the traditional and much-abused tool used to measure hedge fund risk is the *volatility* or *standard deviation* associated with an investment's track record.

Statistically speaking, the standard deviation measures the degree to which an individual probability value varies from the distribution mean—or in plain English, how much a manager's results are dispersed around a central average value. We can see this by looking at the distribution of the returns of the Marsh and Steady Funds in Chart 4.3.

The more volatile a manager's track record, the more unpredictable that manager's returns are considered to be in the future and thus riskier for the investor. This higher volatility translates into a greater dispersion of the manager's returns around an average value. This, in turn, yields us a larger standard deviation in the manager's returns.

Applying the standard deviation to the track records of the Marsh and Steady Funds on the basis of our inspection of Chart 4.3 and from the data in Table 4.1, we would expect the Steady Fund to have a lower standard deviation than the Marsh Fund.

In Table 4.1 we see that the $6^1/_2$-year standard deviation of the Steady Fund is about 90 percent smaller than that of the Marsh Fund, confirming the validity of standard deviation as a proxy for risk.

TABLE 4.1

Marsh and Steady Funds Standard Deviation Statistics, January 1990 to June 1996

	$6^1/_2$-Year Standard Deviation	1-Year Standard Deviation
Steady Fund	0.293761	0.320018
Marsh Fund	3.872945	2.419338

Source: Lara Capital.

CHART 4.3

Distribution of returns for Marsh and Steady Funds from January 1990 to June 1996.

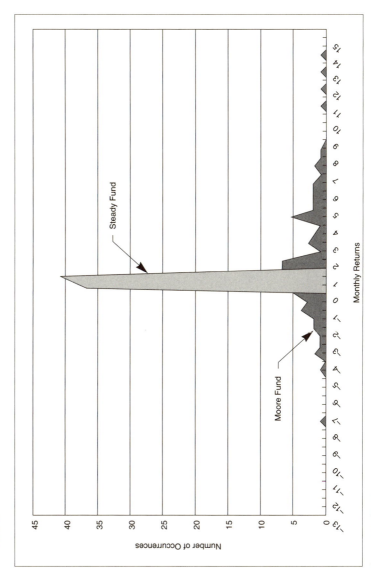

Number of Occurrences

Monthly Returns

Steady Fund

Moore Fund

Source: Lara Capital.

41

However, in Table 4.1 we can also see that by changing the period over which we measure the standard deviation from $6^{1}/_{2}$ years to 1 year, the value of the standard deviation statistic changes. We also note that this change is substantial in both size and direction for each manager. The standard deviation of the Steady Fund increases by 8.9 percent while the standard deviation of the Marsh Fund declines 43 percent. This observation warns us that while standard deviation may be a good proxy for a level of a fund's riskiness, its value is anything but standard. We should exercise caution when comparing standard deviation values between funds, unless we are confident about the comparability and consistency of the underlying data. The value of the standard deviation statistic is strongly influenced by characteristics and length of the track record on which it is based.

RISK: PROBLEMS WITH STATISTICAL MEASUREMENTS

Like any other statistical measure of risk based on historical data, standard deviation is backward-looking. Assuming that the track record accurately represents the manager's investment activities, and assuming that we are using the right tool, the standard deviation statistic tells us that the risk should be X. Should these assumptions continue to hold in the future, we can expect that the fund's standard deviation will continue to be X. Should anything happen to alter this, then all bets are off.

This brings us to a series of important observations regarding the use of quantitative tools in finance. The use of any statistical estimation technique to measure risk will *always* be colored by how we arrive at our risk estimates. In particular, any statistical estimation of risk will always be founded on three key elements, each one of which has the potential to introduce substantial distortions and biases in our results. Given their importance, we should take a closer look at them:

- *Track record.*   We cannot perform any estimation without having data. The distortions a track record can introduce derive from its length and how it was derived and calculated.
- *Assumptions.*   In any analysis we must make assumptions about the track record and on the processes and the techniques we use. These assumptions can include the appropriate length of our track record, the way it was computed, and the repeatability of past performance in the future.
- *Models.*   A model is the tool we use to numerically represent, capture, and predict the event we are trying to measure. Since the real world is too complex to manipulate with the mathematical tools presently at our disposal, any model will be a simplification of reality. The problems introduced by models inevitably revolve around what was left out, that is, the simplifications that have been made to the real world to make the model manageable mathematically.

RISK: PROBLEMS IN APPLYING STATISTICAL TOOLS TO HEDGE FUNDS

Many hedge funds present some special challenges to investors attempting to measure a fund's risk using statistical tools, such as standard deviation. It is not difficult to understand why.

Many hedge funds are dynamic investment vehicles relying on fast positioning and asset turnover to generate their performance. As we saw in the case of the Quantum Fund, statistical tools that do not allow for this dynamic hedge fund behavior will fail to capture and yield meaningful insights. In calculating standard deviation, however, we are simply deriving a static yardstick. First, we are taking all the numbers in a manager's track record to compute an *average* return over the whole track record. In so doing, we are summing good returns to bad ones, and averaging them out. We then take the same return numbers and calculate their dispersion around this average. We are thus collapsing all the manager's performance in a dynamic world into two static numbers: this manager's average return and the standard deviation of these returns. The wide range over which the averages are often calculated tells us little as to what is really going on in the fund, and all the important information is lost in the workings of the underlying averaging process.

One solution to this problem is to calculate average returns and standard deviation statistics using "rolling" data periods. To do this, we perform our calculations on a smaller fixed time period of the track record, starting at the beginning of our track record and then adding and dropping periods as we move forward in time until we reach the end of our track record data. Because our starting and ending points are constantly changing, the value of our standard deviation will change, often substantially. To illustrate this point let us once again use the $6^1/_2$-year track record of the Marsh Fund. In Chart 4.4 we compute the rolling standard deviations over 5-, 4-, 3-, 2-, 1-year and 6-month rolling periods.

As we can see from Chart 4.4, according to the time window used, the standard deviation of the Marsh Fund's returns changes. Additionally, the shorter the period, the more volatile the standard deviations tend to be. This raises the question as to which is the most appropriate time window in which to perform these rolling calculations. Furthermore, as we change time windows, do changes in the manager's standard deviation over time tell us anything about the manager?

The answer to this depends on many factors, such as the frequency with which the NAVs underlying the track record are calculated, the underlying markets in which the manager operates, our understanding of the manager's investment

CHART 4.4

Marsh Fund annualized rolling standard deviations: 5-year to 6-month time horizons from January 1990 to June 1996.

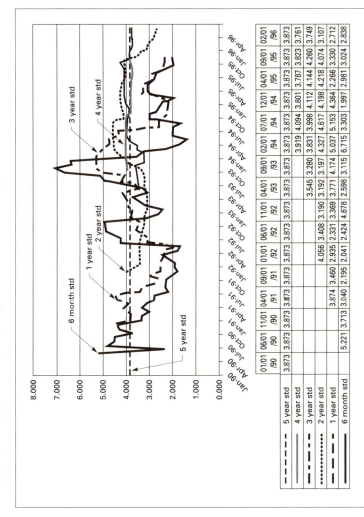

	01/01 /90	06/01 /90	11/01 /90	04/01 /91	09/01 /91	01/01 /92	06/01 /92	11/01 /92	04/01 /93	09/01 /93	02/01 /94	07/01 /94	12/01 /94	04/01 /95	09/01 /95	02/01 /96
5 year std	3.873	3.873	3.873	3.873	3.873	3.873	3.873	3.873	3.873	3.873	3.873	3.873	3.873	3.873	3.873	3.873
4 year std											3.919	4.094	3.801	3.787	3.823	3.761
3 year std									3.545	3.280	3.831	3.998	4.112	4.144	4.260	3.749
2 year std						4.056	3.408	3.190	3.192	3.197	4.327	4.617	4.198	4.218	4.074	3.107
1 year std				3.874	3.460	2.935	2.331	3.369	3.771	4.174	5.037	5.153	4.364	2.266	3.330	2.712
6 month std		5.221	3.713	3.040	2.195	2.041	2.424	4.678	2.598	3.115	6.715	3.303	1.997	2.981	3.024	2.838

Source: Lara Capital.

activities and their directionality, and the amount of trading the manager does. Generally, using monthly NAVs and
quarterly standard deviations appears to provide the best
compromise between data availability and meaningfulness of
the analysis.

As a rule of thumb, we should always derive statistics
using rolling analysis periods of at least two different lengths.
Any sudden, unexpected deviations in the value of the different data sets we derive should be explored in detail with the
manager, as these always tend to be indications of sudden
changes in the manager's activities, or in markets.

RISK: THE HIDDEN ASSUMPTIONS IN USING STANDARD DEVIATION

We have seen that the higher a fund's standard deviation, the
greater its risk for an investor. However, this is not always true.
The validity of this statement depends on the way a manager's
returns are distributed. If a manager's returns follow a normal
distribution, they will be symmetrical, so ranking funds by
means of average returns and standard deviation will give us
meaningful results. However, if the manager's returns are in
any way skewed, then seeking to identify and classify funds
according to average returns and standard deviations will lead
to some incorrect conclusions.

To understand this point better, we'll look at the monthly
pro forma track records of two funds over a $6\frac{1}{2}$-year period, the
Positive and the Negative Funds. From a cursory look at Table
4.2, which presents their average monthly returns and their
standard deviation, we would conclude that the Negative Fund
was a better investment since it has higher average returns and
lower standard deviation than does the Positive Fund. In fact,
the reverse is true. Chart 4.5 clearly illustrates why. The
Positive Fund has a strong positive skew while the Negative
Fund is much more symmetrically distributed.

TABLE 4.2

Annual Standard Deviation Figures for Positive and
Negative Funds: $6^1/_2$-Year Pro Forma Monthly Data

Fund Name	Average Annual Return	Annual Standard Deviation
Positive Fund	1.733333	10.9218
Negative Fund	2.142857	1.409998

Source: Lara Capital.

The presence of skews means that we must distinguish between positive and negative standard deviations and volatility. This is because real-world investors are not indifferent to positive and negative volatility, if the two are not equally likely in outcome. Real-world investors are, in fact, more concerned about losses than gains. For this reason they prefer positive volatility; positive returns greater than the fund's average return are generally welcomed. On the other hand, they seek to avoid negative volatility; negative returns greater than the fund's average returns. Thus, all other things being equal, a fund with high positive volatility will always be more attractive to investors.

In Chart 4.5 the presence of skews means that investors are clearly better off investing in the Positive Fund than the Negative Fund because, while the Positive Fund shows slightly lower average returns of 1.7 versus 2.14 percent, its volatility is both high and entirely positive. By inspecting its distribution we see that the Positive Fund never generated any negative returns for investors in its $6^1/_2$-year history. Assuming that the past is a perfect predictor of a manager's future performance, such a fund is a much better choice, since it has a greater probability of generating positive surprises for its investors.

CHART 4.5

Positive and Negative Funds, showing the effects of skewed data on $6\frac{1}{2}$-year monthly pro forma data.

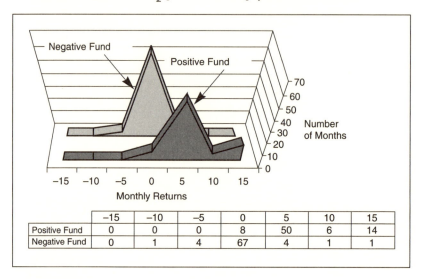

	−15	−10	−5	0	5	10	15
Positive Fund	0	0	0	8	50	6	14
Negative Fund	0	1	4	67	4	1	1

Source: Lara Capital.

If the distributions of hedge fund returns were free from skews, such considerations could be considered as an amusing statistical footnote. The standard assumption is that financial, and thus hedge fund, returns are normally (or log-normally) distributed.[2] This means that, over time, the outcomes follow a symmetrical bell-shaped distribution. In reality, this assumption of normality in the distribution of hedge fund returns is generally incorrect.

---

[2] Appendix 2 contains a review of a normal distribution and its properties.

CHAPTER 5

Hedge Fund Returns

HEDGE FUND RETURNS: DISTRIBUTION CHARACTERISTICS

It is very convenient to assume that hedge fund returns are normally distributed. This assumption allows us to use the distribution's symmetrical properties and a whole host of handy tools (not to mention prepackaged software routines) to make handy predictions about the consistency and stability of a manager's returns, vastly simplifying the mathematical analysis. But is this assumption realistic?

To answer this question, let's return to our data for the Steady and Marsh Funds, and test to see if the distribution of their returns is normally distributed. From the properties of a normal distribution, we should expect that over our $6\frac{1}{2}$-year track record we should have less than two data points (1.5, to be precise) with returns greater or smaller than two standard deviations of the fund's average return. Table 5.1 shows something different.

Table 5.1 seems to imply that the two managers' returns are not conforming to what we would expect from a normal distribution. They are in some way either skewed or flatter or have "fatter tails" than is assumed by the bell shape of a normal distribution. Is nonnormality just a special property of the

TABLE 5.1

Distributions of Returns Theory and Practice for Steady
and Marsh Funds from January 1990 to June 1996

	Marsh Fund			Steady Fund	
Returns	>9.7937 (+2 SD*)	<−5.698 (−2 SD)	Returns	>1.1344 (+2 SD)	<−0.0405 (−2 SD)
Theory	1.56	1.56	Theory	1.56	1.56
Reality	4	1	Reality	0	0

*Standard deviation.
Source: Lara Capital.

Marsh and Steady Funds, or is this a common characteristic in
the universe of hedge funds?

Hedge Fund Returns: Anything but Normally Distributed

We'll start by looking at the monthly return indices of the major
hedge fund grouping that we have previously identified: all
hedge funds, value funds, relative-value funds, and market
directional funds. Let us then contract the distribution of these
returns with the applicable normal distribution. This is shown
in Chart 5.1.

The first thing we notice is the loss "tail" that all these
funds have. It is more frequent than should have been predicted by a normal distribution. The second thing is subtler
to distinguish but is nonetheless present. All the distributions have a positive skew; that is, the frequency of positive
returns is to some degree greater than should have been the
case under the normal distribution. In other words, none of
the returns for these major fund groupings conformed to a
normal distribution. Admittedly, we are among the first to
argue that using such catchall categories to make generalizations doesn't really tell us much because we are throwing

C H A R T   5.1

Theoretical versus actual distribution of monthly hedge fund return indices for the major groupings, January 1994 to December 1998: (*a*) all hedge funds; (*b*) directional hedge funds; (*c*) relative-value hedge funds; (*d*) value hedge funds.

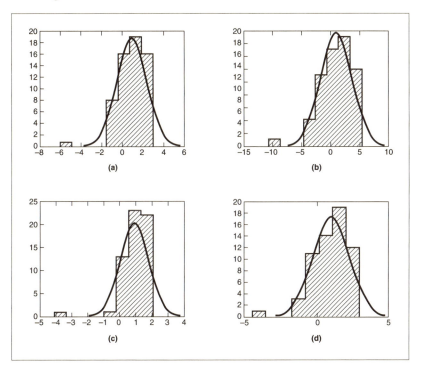

Source: Hfr and Lara Capital.

together all sorts of different manager data. On the other hand, it is important to note that despite this mixing of heterogeneous hedge fund styles and data, none of the distributions we obtained conformed to a normal distribution. This means that despite the "normalizing" effect we would expect from the law of large numbers, there must be some other factor at work which ensures that manager returns are skewed.

At this point the evidence would seem to point to the fact that skewed returns must be an inherent characteristic of hedge funds. This means that we should use caution in assuming normally distributed returns. But why should hedge fund returns be so consistently skewed?

HEDGE FUND RETURNS: PICTURES OF SKILL

Previously we saw that a manager who is less constrained to buy-and-hold investment strategies will more likely see returns that can be independent of the performance of the underlying asset. For this reason, the manager's "skill" becomes more important in generating returns. But what exactly is a manager's investment skill?

In previous chapters we have seen how financial risk and reward are intertwined. We also saw that the balance between financial risk and reward is constantly changing in response to changes in the marketplace (prices, news, investor perceptions, and random acts of nature). Depending on the liquidity, sophistication, and depth of the market, these constant changes can generate substantial, but temporary, mispricings of an investment's risk. We also know that successful hedge funds allegedly try to add value to an investor's portfolio by identifying and exploiting these mispricings. Capturing mispricings is, however, not enough to guarantee success for an investment manager. Successful hedge funds must manage these strategies so as to pass as much of these benefits as possible (after fees, of course) to their investors. This means that we can simplify the issue of manager's skill into two main issues:

- *Prowess*—manager's ability to identify and capitalize on situations that have high reward and lower risk than perceived by the market
- *Risk management*—manager's ability to cut losses and let winners run.

In either case, the net effect of skill on managerial returns should be that these managers will have made more on their winning positions than they will have lost on their losing ones. Although it is fairly easy to understand how investment prowess can skew a manager's returns, risk management is a little harder to understand and warrants further exploration.

HEDGE FUND RETURNS: SKEWS, RISK MANAGEMENT, AND INVESTMENT SKILLS

In its purest form, *risk management* is the art of managing financial risks in such a way as to maximize returns with minimal costs or losses. In today's financial markets, managers have a series of basic tools that they can use to reduce risk.

1. *Close the position outright.*   This means removing exposure to the position. By closing the position, we no longer have any downside—we have covered our risk, but we have no further upside. We have also monetized the paper gain or loss inherent in the position up to that point. In other words, closing a position removes our exposure to a risk at the cost of fixing the gains and losses we had on that position.

2. *Buy protection on the position.*   This means that we transfer the risks inherent in our position to a third party while keeping our underlying position open. In today's financial markets we can accomplish this in any number of ways, using futures, options, swaps, and numerous other financial instruments. However, this transfer of risk is not without cost to us. Parties to whom we transfer our risks will require some form of compensation for the risks they are taking from us. This cost may be greater than, equal to, or smaller than the return we are receiving on the underlying investment. The instrument may also entail other costs represented by limitations on our upside or downside protection.

3. *Buy protection on a related but different position.*   This technique is a different approach to buying protection. The idea behind this technique is quite simple. I may be able to reduce my risks and costs of hedging my underlying position by taking an opposite position in a financial instrument or asset that behaves like my underlying position, but costs me less than a direct hedge. This sounds logical and very nice; however, while this technique may reduce some of my hedging costs, it has done so by adding a different risk to my position. This risk is represented by the degree to which my hedge will track (i.e., behave identically to) my underlying position over time. This tracking or "basis" risk can be substantial, difficult to evaluate a priori, and difficult to manage. A good rule of thumb in evaluating proxy hedges is that if it appears to be much cheaper than a full hedge, then it probably is a poor hedge over time.

4. *Create a portfolio of positions so as to diversify the risk.* This technique is also called *diversification.* In many ways it is the cornerstone of modern portfolio theory and is the basis for many mathematical models of asset management and allocation. For all its mathematical sophistication, diversification is really simply the commonsense rule of not putting all one's eggs in the same basket.

As can be seen, both techniques one and two require us to eliminate or reduce the upside from the investment we are going to hedge. Stated in another way, hedging will always entail a cost. This cost will always reduce our return on the underlying investment. The greater the amount of exposure we hedge, the greater our costs and the lower our returns. So unless one operates in highly inefficient markets, where participants make consistent and continuous pure arbitrage profits, it is almost impossible to be fully hedged consistently and make substantial gains. That does not mean that it is impossible for this to happen from time to time. Financial markets are sufficiently volatile, dynamic, and complex that managers may be able to hedge without costs from time to time. It is improbable in today's markets for such pure arbitrage situations to be consistently available.

In any event, managing positions will require managers to make constant risk/reward tradeoffs, which, in turn, influence the distribution of their returns over time and hence the skew we see in skillful managers.

HEDGE FUND RETURNS: DANGER–"FAT TAILS"

We have seen how managers' skills must influence the distribution of their returns. We suggest that the more skillful the managers, the less likely their returns will be to conform to a normal distribution. To illustrate this point, let's take two investment track records. The first is the Random Fund, a pro forma track record determined by $6^1/_2$ years of random monthly data. These data were created using a random-number generator with values constrained between −10 and +10. The second, the Best Fund, is a composite of the monthly returns of three of the largest and best-known macro hedge fund managers (Jaguar, Moore, and Tudor) during a $6^1/_2$-year period from January 1990 to June 1996. We have selected these two track records, with comparable length and ranges, to illustrate the differences we will encounter when comparing skillful to unskillful managers. Since the Random Fund's returns are not produced by skill, we would expect the distribution of Best Fund's returns to exhibit skews. Chart 5.2 shows the two track records.

Let us now take the data from Chart 5.2 and compare the distribution of these two managers' returns with that of the assumed normal distribution for these returns. The results are shown in Chart 5.3.

Inspecting Chart 5.3, we notice some very important distinctions. First, results of the Random Fund's closely track those of a normal distribution. Those of the Best Fund, however, do not. A close inspection of Chart 5.3 reveals how the distribution is skewed toward the positive. The Best Fund distribution also has the fat tails we saw in Chart 5.1.

CHART 5.2

Monthly returns for Best and Random Funds, January 1990 to June 1996.

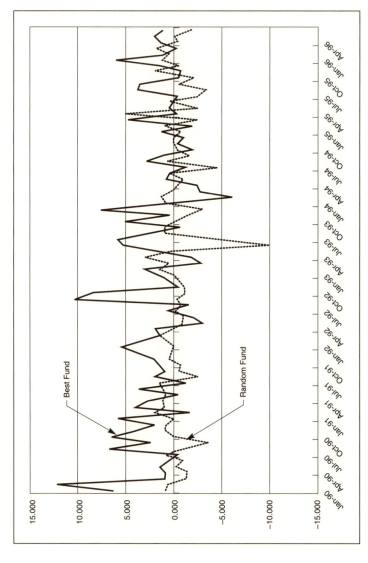

Source: Lara Capital.

CHART 5.3

Best (*a*) and Random (*b*) Funds actual versus theoretical distributions, January 1990 to June 1996.

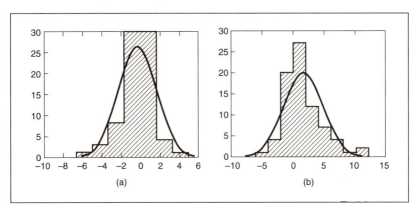

(a)   (b)

Source: Lara Capital.

The term "fat tails" means that exceptional events (large gains or losses) are more frequent than would have been predicted by techniques relying on the assumption of a normal distribution.

This seems to tell us that the returns of a more skillful manager are less likely to look and behave like those of a normal distribution. Thus, the key determinant in the skews and tails in managers' returns are their consistent abilities to find and exploit opportunities that have very highly attractive risk/reward ratios (high reward, low risk), or to manage their positions and risks by cutting their losses and letting their winners run.

At this point it is reasonable to ask if the difference between the actual distribution of Best Fund's returns and those predicted by a normal distribution will have any impact on our assessment of the Best Fund's risk, as measured by the standard deviation (see Table 5.2).

As we can see from Table 5.2, the Random Fund shown in Chart 5.3 has a standard deviation of 1.977 percent versus

TABLE 5.2

Best and Random Funds Average Annual Returns and Standard Deviation Statistics, January 1990 to June 1996

Fund	Average Annual Return, %	Annual Standard Deviation, %
Random Fund	−0.31971	1.703998
Best Fund	1.977884	3.141394

Source: Lara Capital.

the 3.141 percent for the Best Fund. The data in Table 5.2 indicate that the Best Fund is clearly the better choice, since it has higher average returns. But it also appears to be the riskier of the two funds. This is wrong because of the differences in how the distributions are shaped. Going back to Chart 5.3, we see that the Best Fund adds value to its investors by reaping the effects of positive volatility while damping those of the negative volatility. This means that the distribution of its returns is not symmetrical. Winning months outweigh losing ones in both frequency and size. As we have come to expect from such a situation, volatility as measured by standard deviation is a misleading indicator of risk. This raises a problem. If hedge fund returns tend to be skewed and standard deviation is a poor proxy for risk for skewed data, how should we measure risk?

HEDGE FUND RETURNS: THE D RATIO AS AN INDICATOR OF RISK

Using the insight that the skew in a hedge fund's returns contains information on how it is managed, we can derive a powerful tool for evaluating them. We can see that the skew in a hedge fund's returns seems to be connected to the managers' abilities to consistently select high-reward, low-risk opportunities, manage their investments with uncommon skill, or both. Returning to the Best Fund we reviewed in the previous section, we'll replot the distribution of this manager's returns in Chart 5.4 to eliminate the number of zero monthly returns.

The distributions of the Best Fund's returns now fall into two camps. Those greater than zero are indicated by the letter *A*. Those less than zero are indicated by the letter *B*. Multiplying *A* and *B*, we obtain the value of the two areas under the nonzero parts of the curve. The ratio of these two areas gives us a parameter, which essentially compares the value and frequency of the manager's winners to losers. Essentially, this statistic captures the curve's skew, and can thus be used as a proxy for a manager's skill. At the same time,

CHART 5.4

Best Fund distribution of monthly returns, with zero return months removed, January 1990 to June 1996.

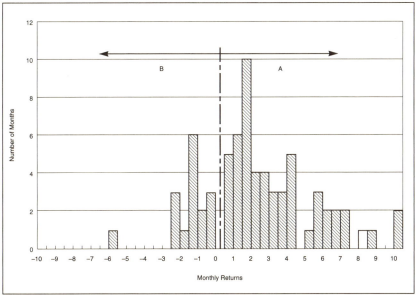

Source: Lara Capital.

because a manager's skill determines the true risk we face as investors in the fund, it can be used as a proxy for a fund's risk. This statistic, which we shall define as the *d ratio*, is computed as follows:

$$d \text{ ratio} = \text{Abs} \frac{d}{U}$$

where d = number of returns less than zero* their value[1]
    U = number of returns greater than zero* their value
  Abs = absolute value (i.e., we ignore the negative value, if any, of d)

As we saw in Chart 5.4, the more skewed the curve, the greater a manager's skill. Likewise, the lower the value of the d ratio, the more skillful a manager. In particular, the d ratio will have a value between 0 and infinity. A d ratio of 0 is a distribution of returns that has no downside. A d ratio of 1 is a perfectly equal distribution of returns around 0. A d ratio of infinity is one whose manager cannot generate positive returns for investors. In general, the lower a manager's d ratio, the more attractive the manager is. Conversely, the higher a manager's d ratio, the less attractive the manager is. Finally, a d ratio of 1 should be considered a red flag, as the manager may not be bringing any value-added assets to our portfolio.

One convenience of the d ratio is that it makes no assumptions about the underlying distribution of returns. This allows us to rank and sort managers in terms of the true value they bring to an investor's portfolio.

Let us now look at the d ratio in action by compiling a ranking of the major hedge fund indices based on both standard deviation and the d ratio. The results are shown in Table 5.3.

---

[1] The star represents the multiplication operator, i.e., returns less than zero times their value.

TABLE 5.3

Major Hedge Fund Indices (in Percent) Sorted by Annual
Standard Deviation and D-Ratio Statistics, January 1994
to December 1998

Sorting by D Ratio	D Ratio	Standard Deviation	Sorting by Standard Deviation	D Ratio	Standard Deviation
Relative value	0.00	2.59	Market-neutral	1.22	1.94
Convertible arbitrage	0.00	2.66	Relative value	0.00	2.59
Merger	0.08	2.61	Merger	0.08	2.61
Distressed	0.28	3.87	Convertible arbitrage	0.00	2.66
Mortgage	0.43	3.40	Mortgage	0.43	3.40
Market-neutral	1.22	1.94	Distressed	0.28	3.87
Market timing	1.42	4.07	Market timing	1.42	4.07
Equity hedge	1.58	5.41	Event-driven	3.33	4.40
Event-driven	3.33	4.40	Equity hedge	1.58	5.41
Macro	6.79	5.51	Macro	6.79	5.51
Emerging market	11.54	10.51	Emerging market	11.54	10.51

Source: Hfr and Lara Capital.

CHAPTER 6

Hedge Fund Leverage

LEVERAGE: A DOUBLE-EDGED SWORD

As we saw, leverage is one of the defining elements of a hedge fund's operations. It is also an important component of their returns and the additional benefits or value added they bring to investors. But exactly what is hedge fund leverage, and why is it so important for hedge funds and their returns?

In simple terms, *hedge fund leverage* is the value of assets or positions a fund has over and above its capital. The larger the notional or market value of a fund's positions over its investor supplied capital, the greater the fund's leverage. A fund with U.S. $50,000,000 in capital and U.S. $60,000,000 of positions has a leverage of 1.2:1. This means that for every U.S. $1 of capital the fund has, it has open positions in the market with a value of $1.2. The U.S. $10,000,000 extra the fund has in positions over its capital is the amount the fund has borrowed. A fund's leverage is thus directly related to the amount of money that it has borrowed to finance positions larger than its capital.

By allowing managers to increase the size of their positions, leverage allows managers to magnify their returns. Since many hedge fund managers are paid on the basis of performance, the greater the leverage, the greater the fund's potential returns and performance fees. Overleveraging to boost fees is often a powerful temptation for some hedge fund managers. As we'll see, this problem is often the most serious in funds of funds, where it is often harder to detect.

To understand how leverage increases returns, we will use the case of a fund with U.S. $50,000,000 in capital which invests in one position, under different market and leverage assumptions. Table 6.1 demonstrates a manager's performance under these different assumptions.

From Table 6.1, we see how a 5 percent gain on the manager's position, if leveraged 2:1, nets the manager U.S. $5,000,000, a return of 10 percent on initial capital. A 10 percent gain on the manager's position, if leveraged 3:1, nets the manager U.S. $15,000,000, an impressive return of 30 percent on initial capital. In other words, leveraging allows returns to be magnified. However, it is a double-edged sword. Leverage magnifies both investment returns and losses. Looking again at Table 6.1, we notice the impact it has on a manager's performance in a falling market. If the manager's position loses 5 percent while leveraged at 2:1, the manager will have a loss of U.S. $5,000,000, equal to 10 percent of initial capital. A 10 percent loss on the manager's position, leveraged at 3:1, results in a loss of U.S. $15,000,000, or the equivalent of 30 percent of initial capital. This translates as a substantial blow for any fund.

In the history of investing, some investors have succeeded in using leverage in excess of 50:1. However, few have successfully used such high leverage consistently for long periods of time, because of the way it can magnify even minor adverse price moves. This was clearly evidenced in the case of Long-Term Capital Management, where high leverage magnified relatively minor but unexpected negative price moves and accelerated the firm's collapse in the summer of 1998. Excessive or injudicious leverage is, in fact, the major cause of hedge fund losses in volatile or falling markets. As we shall see later, the technical aspects of leverage often further increase this downside effect in a way that is not symmetrical to the magnification effect that leverage gives on the upside, adding to the dangers of leverage in adverse markets.

TABLE 6.1

The Impact of Leverage on Fund Performance

Capital U.S. $50,000,000	Position Increases 5% in Value	Position Decreases 5% in Value	Position Increases 10% in Value	Position Decreases 10% in Value
Leverage 1:1, notional position value U.S. $50,000,000	Gain U.S. $2,500,000	Loss U.S. $2,500,000	Gain U.S. $5,000,000	Loss U.S. $5,000,000
Leverage 2:1, notional position value U.S. $100,000,000	Gain U.S. $5,000,000	Loss U.S. $5,000,000	Gain U.S. $10,000,000	Loss U.S. $10,000,000
Leverage 3:1, notional position value U.S. $150,000,000	Gain U.S. $7,500,000	Loss U.S. $7,500,000	Gain U.S. $15,000,000	Loss U.S. $15,000,000

Despite its potential risks, leverage per se is neither inherently good nor bad. When used well and judiciously, it is merely another, albeit very powerful, investment management tool, which can increase a manager's flexibility and ability to capture favorable market moves.

LEVERAGE AS AN INVESTMENT TOOL

Like all other effective investors, hedge fund managers need to ask themselves the following seven questions:

1. What should I buy—what is my position or exposure going to be?
2. How should I buy it—what instrument should I use to obtain the exposure I desire?
3. What is my time horizon—how long should I hold my investment for?
4. When should I sell—what is my profit target on this investment?
5. What is my stop loss—what is the maximum amount of loss I'm willing to take on this investment?
6. How much should I buy—how much leverage should I use?
7. What percentage of my portfolio should be in this investment—how much leverage should I have in my overall portfolio?

As we see from this list, leverage can become a crucial component at two points in this investment decision process: at the position level (how much should I buy) and at the portfolio level (how large should my portfolio be to accommodate my purchase). Depending on how they are addressed, these issues can have a considerable impact on a manager's portfolio and its risk/reward profile. Before reviewing this point, first we need to understand the mechanics of how hedge funds can create leverage.

HOW HEDGE FUNDS CREATE LEVERAGE

We have seen that leverage is determined by managers' abilities to borrow money to buy positions for an amount greater than their fund's capital. In today's markets there are many ways managers can do this. For the sake of simplicity, we break them down into four main groups or types:

- Uncollateralized loans
- Collateralized loans
- Margin accounts
- Instruments with embedded leverage

Let's look at these leverage tools in turn to understand how they work and what they could imply for an investor.

Uncollateralized Loans

As a freestanding company, a hedge fund manager can present the fund's financial information to a bank and ask for a loan on the basis of its past performance and expected revenues. To secure this loan, the fund uses only its financial strength as shown by balance sheet and income statements, without pledging any of its assets. Only the largest, best-known funds succeed in obtaining these types of loans.

Secured Loans

To secure a loan, a hedge fund will pledge an asset (financial or other) to the lending bank, in addition to providing financial information on its operations. The value of the loan, depending on the liquidity, marketability, and safety of the collateral, will be some fraction of the collateral. A loan secured by a high-quality liquid security such as U.S. Treasury bills is typically for about 95 percent of the face value of the collateral. In other words, by pledging one dollar's worth of high-quality securities, a fund can obtain a loan of 95¢. The 5¢ difference is often called a "haircut" and is the margin of safety lenders believe will protect them should they be forced to sell the collateral to repay the loan in the event of a fund default. In general, the more illiquid or the poorer the credit grades of the security, the higher the haircut, and so the smaller the amount loaned by the bank. At this point it is important to understand that the lender is often the sole arbiter of both the value of the collateral, and more importantly the amount of the haircut. Furthermore, values are not constant and can be changed at any point during the life of the loan, at the lender's discretion.

Whenever the value assigned to the collateral falls below a level established by the bank, the fund will be asked to "top up" or add more cash or securities to its collateral with the bank. Should the fund be unable to do so following such a request, once again the bank can call the loan, sell the collateral position, and sue the fund for any shortfall.

Margin Accounts

Stocks, futures, and other derivatives can be bought via a margin account. A margin account is a variation of a secured loan, used to finance positions in financial instruments. In one form or another margin lending is present in all the major financial markets, from stocks and bonds to derivatives and foreign exchange. Its form and practices may vary from market to market, depending on market conventions and regulations.

Under a basic margin loan a broker or some other financial intermediary finances a fund's asset purchase[1] through a loan secured by the asset itself, and cash (or other highly liquid, high-quality securities). The cash amount or *margin* is generally determined by the security's *market risk*, a statistically based estimate of its future volatility. In other words, margins are determined by how much brokers feel the value of the security could change should they have to sell it to cover their loans. On

---

[1]For simplicity, we consider the case of a purchase, but the same mechanism will hold true for asset sales done on margin.

top of this amount, brokers generally add an extra layer of protection determined by internal credit guidelines and local regulatory requirements. For stocks in the United States, the National Association of Securities Dealers (NASD) and New York Stock Exchange (NYSE) require a minimum margin of 25 percent of the value of the security. This means that sophisticated investors can obtain a leverage ratio of around 4:1 on U.S. blue chip stocks; that is, for every dollar of collateral they can hold $4.00 in positions. For other assets, depending on the asset, the market, the broker, and the applicable regulations, the hedge fund manager can obtain leverage ranging from 5:1 to 20:1. Unlike a secured loan, the value of the position and the collateral are measured at least daily, and in many cases in real time, depending on the prevailing market prices. Although the pricing of the collateral is less arbitrary than in the case of a collateralized loan, the brokers financing the position still have the right to raise or change margin requirements at any time and at their discretion.

Instruments

Many types of derivatives allow a manager to take positions whose payoff replicates the value of a leveraged position in the cash market. These instruments allow the manager to circumvent all the problems of opening and managing a margin account, since in essence this responsibility is transferred to the financial intermediary that issued or structured the instrument.

Pyramiding and Hiding Leverages

Using these building blocks, hedge fund managers can weave leverage into different aspects of their operations. This flexibility often allows hedge fund managers to hide the amount of leverage they are using from both their investors and lenders.

A classic example of how this can be done is shown in Table 6.2, where a U.S. $50,000,000 fund borrows U.S. $1,000,000 via an unsecured bank loan to purchase government bonds. It then pledges the bonds to another bank as collateral for a loan with a 10 percent haircut. Finally, it uses the proceeds of the second loan to purchase a structured note having a payoff equivalent to the original bonds it purchased but leveraged at 3:1. Through these operations, the manager has transformed a U.S. $1,000,000 position in government bonds, into a position with a market exposure to the same bonds equivalent to U.S. $5,700,000, representing a 470 percent increase in market exposure.

As we can see from Table 6.2, only one-third of the fund's leverage can be readily determined on the basis of its bank borrowings. The remainder of the fund's leveraged is "hidden" by being contained in the structured note it is holding in its investment portfolio.

Hidden leverage is one of the reasons why hedge fund credit information clearinghouses will never be an effective way of policing hedge fund leverage. Theoretically, these exchanges should help detect poorly run, overleveraged hedge funds. However, the temptations of hidden leverage are just too great and hedge fund managers will always find ways of hiding their leverage to circumvent these reporting obligations.

One area in which hidden leverage is particularly endemic and harmful for investors is a fund of funds. Many banks are willing to take hedge fund shares as collateral for loans. This allows fund-of-fund promoters to pyramid their leverage in a mechanism akin to that outlined in Table 6.2, summing the leverage inherent in the fund operations to that provided by the bank, via the pledged shares. This type of leverage is attractive for fund-of-fund promoters, as it boosts the fund's returns, and offsets effects of the hedge fund promoter's fees (which are in addition to those of the underlying fund) on performance. The effective market exposures that some of these fund-of-fund structures entail for investors can be quite terrifying, often exceeding 50:1 once all the different components and levels of leverage are unraveled.

TABLE 6.2

Pyramiding Leverage

	Fund Assets, U.S. $	Borrowings, U.S. $	Collateral, U.S. $	Fund's Market Exposure, U.S. $	Ratio of Market Exposure to Fund Assets, %
Initial capital	50,000,000				
Unsecured loan		1,000,000	0	51,000,000	2.00
Secured loan		900,000	100,000	51,900,000	3.80
Structured note (3:1 leverage)				55,700,000	11.40

Conclusion

In reviewing some of the mechanical aspects of leverage, note the power and discretion that leveraged managers gave to their lenders in exchange for the loan. It is this power that lenders have which results in a de facto asymmetry between leverage risks and rewards in the real world.

UNSYMMETRICAL RISK/REWARD PROFILES WITH LEVERAGE

A prudent lender will always try to ensure the repayment of a loan. This means that the valuation of collateral will depend on prevailing market conditions and will not be symmetrical with respect to similar-sized moves in up and down markets. Specifically, lenders will always tend to assign lower valuations to collateral when market conditions are the most difficult. This increases their protection and reduces the amount of leverage a fund will be able to carry. This will always occur when a fund has the least liquidity, thereby forcing funds to close positions to raise cash and pay down their loans and/or meet margin calls. The net effect of this process is that leverage forces funds to monetize losses faster in falling markets than they would in rising markets, adversely affecting their performance.

This is a complex issue to grasp, so we'll use a few examples based on the working of the Hapless Fund, a hypothetical hedge fund with U.S. $1,000,000 in capital raised from investors.

We'll start by assuming that the Hapless Fund uses its U.S. $1,000,000 capital to buy a 5-year U.S. Treasury note at 100. This note is then used as collateral by a bank for a U.S. $500,000 loan (i.e., the bank's haircut is 50 percent). Finally, the loan proceeds are used to buy more of the same note. The net results of these transactions is to allow the Hapless Fund to increase the notional value of its positions from U.S. $1,000,000 to $1,500,000, giving it a leverage of 1.5:1. Table 6.3 shows the results of these transactions of the balance sheet of the Hapless Fund.

T A B L E   6.3

Hapless Fund Pro Forma Balance Sheet, Basic Position

Assets, U.S. $		Liabilities, U.S. $	
Collateral with bank	1,000,000	Loans	500,000
Additional position	500,000	Change in collateral value	0
		Revaluation of investments	0
		Initial equity	1,000,000
Total assets	1,500,000	Total liabilities	1,500,000

Having set up the Hapless Fund's basic position, we see that the bank's loan is secured with a collateral:loan ratio of 2:1; thus, thanks to the 50 percent haircut, it has twice the amount of collateral of its loan exposure. In reviewing Table 6.3, we also see how the Hapless Fund is exposed to changes in interest rates. Specifically, if *interest rates fall, the fund will make money* because its investments in treasury notes will increase in value. If *interest rates rise, the fund will lose money* because its investments in treasury notes will decrease in value. Let's work through these two cases to see how the rise and fall in interest rates will affect the Hapless Fund's performance.

1. *Interest rates fall 5 percent.* The price of the notes goes from 100 to 105. The value of the investment positions at the Hapless Fund rise from U.S. $1,500,000 to $1,575,000. Because bonds have risen in price, the value of the collateral the Hapless Fund has deposited with the bank has also increased, going from U.S. $500,000 to $525,000. This leaves the Hapless Fund with U.S. $25,000 of excess collateral with the bank, which it could theoretically withdraw and use to buy more bonds. The effects of these transactions on the balance sheet of the Hapless Fund are shown in Table 6.4.

The rise in asset prices has increased the bank collateral:loan ratio from 2:1 to 2.1:1. Because the market has risen, the bank has no problem in releasing back to the Hapless

TABLE 6.4

Hapless Fund Pro Forma Balance Sheet in a Rising
Market

Assets, U.S. $		Liabilities, U.S. $	
Collateral with bank	1,050,000	Loans	500,000
Additional position	525,000	Change in collateral value	25,000
		Revaluation of investments	50,000
		Initial equity	1,000,000
Total assets	1,575,000	Total liabilities	1,575,000

Fund the U.S. $25,000 in excess collateral on its books. In so
doing, the bank's collateral loan ratio goes from 2.1:1 to 2.05:1.
In other words, a rising market has effectively enhanced the
bank's credit position.

   2. Interest rates rise 5 percent.   The price of the notes goes
from 100 to 95. The value of investment positions at the Hapless
Fund go from U.S. $1,500,000 to $1,425,000. At the same time,
the value of its collateral with the bank goes from U.S. $500,000
to $475,000. All other things being equal, the Hapless Fund is
now undermargined by U.S. $25,000. The Hapless Fund will
now either have to send the bank extra cash or sell off its collateral, now worth only U.S. $950,000, to repay its $500,000
loan. The effect of these transactions on the balance sheet of the
Hapless Fund are shown in Table 6.5.

   One of the first things we notice in looking at Table 6.5
is that the bank's collateral:loan ratio has gone from 2:1 to
1.9:1. However, even if the Hapless Fund sent in the additional U.S. $25,000 needed to bring the value of its collateral
back to U.S. $500,000, the bank's collateral-to-loan ratio only
improved marginally from 1.90:1 to 1.95:1. In other words, to
keep its credit exposure constant (i.e., the value of the haircut
at U.S. $500,000), the bank must ask the Hapless Fund to send
in an additional U.S. $12,820. This means that in response to
a 5 percent decline in the market, the Hapless Fund must add

TABLE 6.5

Hapless Fund Pro Forma Balance Sheet in a Falling
Market

Assets, U.S. $		Liabilities, U.S. $	
Collateral with bank	950,000	Loans	500,000
Additional position	475,000	Change in collateral value	−25,000
		Revaluation of investments	−50,000
		Initial equity	1,000,000
Total assets	1,425,000	Total liabilities	1,425,000

7.56 percent of its asset's value to keep the banks' credit exposure constant. In other words, the Hapless Fund must now
cover a 51 percent increase in collateral over the market
decline.

We have now seen how declines in the value of a fund may
be far greater than the decline determined by market prices. In
falling markets, it is easy to see how things can spiral out of control. In response to the first price decline, marginal players with
high leverage and low cash may be forced to sell positions at a
loss to raise money to repay their loans or meet margin calls.
This selling can in turn force the market down further. The additional decline may cause other banks to raise their collateral
requirements, in turn forcing other managers with the same
position to sell. The unwinding of leveraged positions can
quickly cause a ripple effect that can move through the market,
forcing an increasing number of investors who owned the same
position on a leveraged basis to sell.

This mechanism of magnified, downward price movements
of assets in falling markets is not a theoretical abstraction. The sudden, sharp price drops that occurred in October 1987, September
1994, and August 1998 are strongly tied to the effects of such sys-
temic margin calls on leveraged players in the markets.

We have looked at how leverage is particularly damag-
ing to hedge funds in falling markets. We have also seen that

it is not always possible to detect leverage just from looking at the amount of loans or margined securities that a hedge fund has on its books. Thus, we need to find some other way of detecting leverage and its potential impact on hedge fund performance.

CHAPTER 7

Detecting Leverage in Hedge Funds

DETECTING LEVERAGE: SHADOWS ON A WALL

Given the importance of leverage in the hedge fund universe and its often elusive nature, it is crucial for investors to find some way of detecting it and measuring its use.

Detecting leverage in a mutual fund is relatively easy. Mutual fund returns are strongly determined by the performance of the underlying asset in which the fund is invested. Thus, returns substantially in excess of the returns of the underlying asset must be the result of leverage. Furthermore, the increase in the downside volatility of the fund's returns over that of the underlying asset will be an indication of how effectively leverage is being used. In other words, the greater a mutual fund's d ratio compared to the asset's d ratio, the less effectively leverage is being used.

With hedge funds, this approach is harder. Since skill is the key determinant of the hedge fund's returns, there is seldom any unique underlying asset in which the fund invests. Furthermore, many funds can rotate their risk books with amazing speed. Because of this, any careful attempt to analyze and monitor leverage is complicated by having to obtain clear, accurate, and exhaustive data on all the manager's positions.

Confronted with the limited data and transparency of the hedge fund world, it would be tempting to say that our task is impossible. In reality, provided we are willing to live with some rough approximations, detecting leverage in a hedge fund is not too complex. To understand how this can be done, we might think of the process as trying to determine the shape of an object we cannot see by the shadows it casts on a wall. Once we have information on the light source and the wall, we can get a pretty good idea of the object's shape.

Independently of its source or form, leverage will always leave a clear mark on the way a manager's returns are distributed. Although it may be possible to hide some of the mechanical aspects of leverage, it is not possible to hide its effects. With this in mind, we can use the distribution of a fund's returns to identify the amount of leverage that may be present in the fund. These are the shadows cast on the wall by the unknown leverage in a fund.

DETECTING LEVERAGE: MEASURING ITS EFFECTIVE USE

As an investor reviewing a fund that uses leverage, one of the first things I want to know is how effectively the leverage is being used. We know that leverage magnifies a fund's gains and losses. Thus, one way to see if a fund uses leverage successfully is to determine whether leverage allowed the fund to increase its gains more than proportionately to its losses. In other words, managers who use leverage effectively will see returns on their winning positions much greater than those on their losing ones. As a first approximation, we can use managers' returns over a risk-free interest rate.[1] In other words, a manager's excess returns over the applicable U.S. Treasury bill (T-bill) rate gives us an idea of the additional investment risks that managers may be incurring. Thus, taking a manager's

---

[1]For a discussion of risk-free rates, please see Appendix 5.

track record, and subtracting the applicable T-bill yield for the period, allows us to derive both the additional return and risk that the manager is bringing to our portfolio.

However, just looking at the manager's incremental risk and returns over the T-bill rate doesn't provide us with sufficient information on the value-added a manager is bringing to our investment portfolio. If we are running a complex portfolio, what we really want to do is evaluate the value-added a manager can bring with respect to a specific asset class. This requires us to compare the manager's return and risk to those of other funds involved in the same type of activity and using the same kind of strategy.

Clearly this approach assumes that we are able to identify a comparable peer group or an acceptable index to represent the manager's peer group. At this point, for the sake of simplicity, let us assume that we have succeeded. The determination of the excess rates is quite straightforward. Once again we take our manager's track record, and from that subtract the applicable return from the index. By looking at the properties of this adjusted distribution, we can gain an understanding of how much a manager may be leveraged, and how effectively that manager is using this leverage.

DETECTING LEVERAGE: A PRACTICAL EXAMPLE

Using as an example two fund managers[2] whom our firm was recently asked to evaluate, we'll apply the concepts we have developed so far. Chart 7.1 shows the cumulative returns of two U.S. equity hedge funds the two managers generated from their 18-year track record.

From Chart 7.1 it would appear that fund 2 is the better investment, as it has consistently provided investors with better average annual returns over its track record. However, by

---

[2]Names are withheld at the managers' request.

CHART 7.1

Two U.S. equity hedge fund managers, cumulative returns from December 1984 to December 1998.

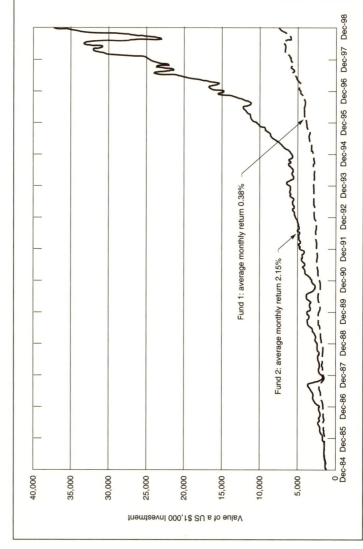

Source: Lara Capital.

CHART 7.2

Two U.S. equity hedge fund managers, return distributions from December 1984 to December 1998.

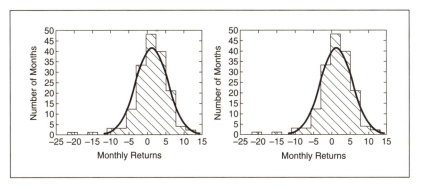

Source: Lara Capital.

now we are savvy enough to ignore cumulative data, and focus on how these returns are distributed over time. These results are reproduced in Chart 7.2.

Surprisingly, as hedge fund managers, funds 1 and 2 both show returns that are almost skewless and conform closely to those of the superimposed normal distribution shown in Chart 7.2. However, the returns do present negative outliners, or fatter negative tails, which means that the managers have the potential to generate additional negative surprises, with a frequency greater than we would expect on the basis of a standard deviation estimate which assumed a normal distribution.

Let us now adjust our return numbers for the risk-free rate and a peer group benchmark. Since both managers are U.S. equity managers, we will use the S&P 500 index as our peer group benchmark. We will then use a total return index based on the U.S. 3-month U.S. Treasury bill as our risk-free rate. Chart 7.3 shows the distributions we obtain after these adjustments.

As we can see from Chart 7.3, the fund 1 peer- and risk-adjusted returns are zero. This manager does not generate any value-added with respect to the S&P 500 index. It is, therefore, a safe assumption to conclude that this investment portfolio is

CHART 7.3

Two U.S. equity hedge fund managers, risk- and peer-group-adjusted return distributions from December 1984 to December 1998.

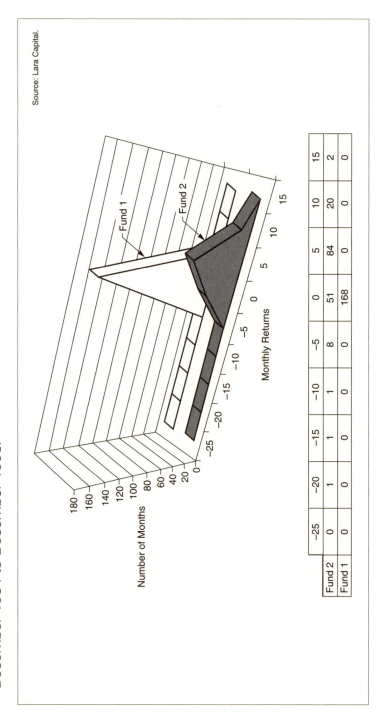

Source: Lara Capital.

	−25	−20	−15	−10	−5	0	5	10	15
Fund 2	0	1	1	1	8	51	84	20	2
Fund 1	0	0	0	0	0	168	0	0	0

either directly or indirectly indexed to the S&P 500, and comparable to the S&P index itself.

The peer- and risk-adjusted returns for fund 2 are more interesting. Once again we note a heavy concentration of investment returns around zero, indicating a heavy linkage of the manager's returns to the S&P 500 index and some tails. To get a better understanding of this distribution, we can recompute the distribution shown in Chart 7.3 to derive its d ratio and contrast the distribution of its returns with a normal distribution. The result of these calculations is shown in Chart 7.4.

Fund 2 has a d ratio of 13 percent, confirming a strong negative skew. However, from Chart 7.4 we also see that the balance of the distribution follows that of a normal distribution with a zero mean. These factors allow us to draw the following conclusions:

- The fund's performance is heavily indexed to the S&P 500, as evidenced by the heavy concentration of adjusted data around zero.
- The fund has a high loss potential as shown by the negative tails.
- The fund's returns contain an X factor that appears to amplify the distribution of returns around zero.

In other words, fund 2 is heavily invested in something that tracks the S&P 500 but contains an X factor. A detailed due-diligence analysis revealed that this X factor was leverage. Our due-diligence analysis revealed that the second manager was investing in a closed-end fund vehicle that specialized in highly leveraged speculation on the S&P 500 futures contract. In other words, fund 2 was using its investment in the closed-end fund to hide leverage. Thanks to the investment in the closed-end fund, fund 2 had a total effective exposure to the S&P 500 index comparable to what it would have obtained with 2:1 leverage, while formally having no debt (and thus leverage) on its books.

As our example showed, interesting clues can be learned from the analysis of a manager's distribution. We also confirmed

CHART 7.4

Fund 2 distribution of returns, risk- and peer-group-adjusted, from December 1984 to December 1998.

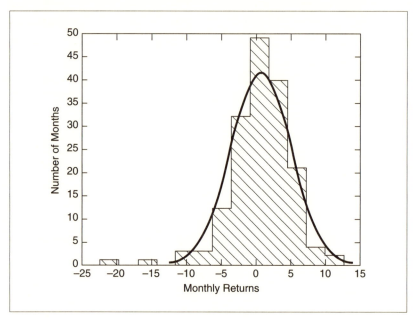

Source: Lara Capital.

the link between the value-added a manager can bring and the shape of the distribution of that manager's returns. In the following chapters we explore other ways in which skill and the distribution of a manager's returns are tied together, uncovering other interesting insights into hedge fund operations and additional tools that can be used to evaluate managers.

As was expected, funds are ranked differently. Unsurprisingly, the funds which show the greatest changes in rank are ones that come from the value and relative-value categories. As we showed in Chart 5.1, these were the categories with the greatest skews. It is also interesting to note two other things that would not have been apparent using a standard deviation statistic:

- The *d* ratio flags market-neutral, market timing, and equity hedge funds as unattractive, offering low value-added.
- The *d* ratio flags relative-value and convertible arbitrage funds as attractive.

It would seem that the *d* ratio can give us as much information as a standard deviation statistic. At the same time, the different assumptions on which it is based can give us more interesting information about a manager.

As powerful as the *d* ratio is, it tells us little about the risks managers take in generating their returns. To derive such information we need to identify how much risk managers actually take, both in absolute terms and in terms of their peers. To do this, we first need to develop an understanding of leverage, since it is the key ingredient of many hedge fund strategies. Leverage is also the greatest source of many fund's returns as well, as it is the greatest source of risk for an investor.

CHAPTER 8

Randomness As a Source of Risk in Hedge Funds

RANDOMNESS: LUCK AND NORMAL DISTRIBUTION OF RETURNS

In seeking valued-added from a hedge fund investment, investors want to have the confidence that it can have a lasting impact on their portfolios. This means they need to distinguish between funds where the returns are generated by a manager's skill, and those that are generated by luck.

When luck determines a manager's performance, its transitory nature robs investors of the assurance that it will be consistent and repeatable. On the other hand, skillful investment managers have something unique which assures their success. Whatever it is—idiosyncratic style, investment disciplines, market know-how, or superior quantitative skills—it will entail consistent biases toward risk and leverage in their activities that will show up clearly as skews in their returns. Just as most individuals tend to have relatively stable personality traits over time, these skill-related traits in an investment manager tend to remain stable over time,[1] giving investors a better chance of consistent and repeatable future performance.

---

[1] This is not to say that paranoid schizophrenics could not make good investment managers, just that since they tend to have a hard time raising money from investors, their track records are very rare, making this claim difficult to disprove.

In Chapter 6 we saw how leverage and skill influence the distribution of a manager's returns. In particular, we saw the way investment skill could cause a manager's returns to deviate from a normal distribution. This led us to make the claim that managers who exhibited normally distributed returns generally provided investors with little value-added because they showed few investment skills in generating their returns. To substantiate this claim we first need to gain an understanding of random events.

RANDOMNESS AND RANDOM EVENTS

A *random event* is essentially something unpredictable a priori. The classic example of a random event is the toss of a coin, or the "market" example outlined in App. 2 and reproduced in Table 8.1.

As we can see from the table, the market during this period was up for 33 days out of 60 (i.e., it was up 55.7 percent of the time). The average return for the period was 0.05, and the total return to an investor in this market would have been 3. Although such a market has a very slight positive skew, a normal distribution with a mean of 0.05 and a standard deviation of 1.43 can approximate it quite well.[2]

A fund whose returns depend on the direction of this market (rather than the manager's skill) to generate the bulk of its returns will have returns that track this market; in other words, they will have a normal distribution with average returns and a standard deviation comparable to those of the underlying market.

Although the average return over the period was expected to be 0.5, a manager who was fully invested in the market illustrated in Table 4.1 would have had a total return of 3 at the end of the period. This return is well in excess of the average

---

[2] Readers unfamiliar with a normal distribution are referred to App. 2 for a brief presentation.

TABLE 8.1

A Randomly Distributed Market Over 60 Periods

Day	Direction	Move	Day	Direction	Move	Day	Direction	Move
1	Down	−1	21	Down	−1	41	Up	0
2	Down	−2	22	Down	−1	42	Up	2
3	Down	−1	23	Down	−1	43	Up	2
4	Up	1	24	Up	1	44	Down	−1
5	Up	0	25	Down	−1	45	Up	1
6	Up	2	26	Up	1	46	Down	−1
7	Down	−2	27	Down	−1	47	Up	0
8	Up	1	28	Up	2	48	Down	−2
9	Up	2	29	Down	−1	49	Up	1
10	Up	0	30	Down	−1	50	Up	1
11	Down	−2	31	Down	−1	51	Down	−1
12	Up	1	32	Down	−2	52	Up	2
13	Down	−2	33	Up	2	53	Down	−1
14	Up	2	34	Down	−2	54	Up	2
15	Up	0	35	Up	1	55	Down	−2
16	Up	0	36	Up	2	56	Down	−1
17	Up	1	37	Up	0	57	Down	−2
18	Down	−1	38	Up	1	58	Up	2
19	Down	−1	39	Up	1	59	Down	−2
20	Up	2	40	Up	1	60	Up	2

expected return over the period. Furthermore, during the 60-day period that manager's returns would have swung between a maximum of +5 and a minimum of −6. These shorter-term fluctuations are due to the size and frequency of the short-term successions of up and down periods in the market, also called *random runs.*

One of the most effective ways of analyzing luck is to think of it as a by-product of these random runs. Since random runs are present in any random event, like a financial market, luck can be regarded as simply an inherent property of investing. An inspection of Table 4.1 confirms that these lucky random runs are inevitably short-lived, meaning that their impact on a manager's performance must be transitory unless bolstered by a manager's skill.

RANDOMNESS: DISTRIBUTION OF RETURNS, PICTURES OF SKILL

We now need to prove our claim that a manager's skill generates consistent returns with stable and predictable skews.

In previous chapters we saw how managers' skills were reflected in the distribution of their returns, in the form of distinctive tails or skews. This analysis had been conducted on the basis of the information contained in the entire track record, throwing all our data into one pot, so to speak. Proving that skillful managers have stable skews means essentially looking at the dynamics of a manager's d ratio over time. This means looking at smaller subperiods in the track record, and calculating a d ratio using the rolling-window technique described earlier. In applying this technique we do not expect to find that skillful managers will have constant d ratios. What we are looking for instead are d ratios that fluctuate within some very predictable and stable levels as a sign of manager skill. In a world of dynamic and complex markets, it is extremely difficult for investment managers to avoid being influenced by outside or random events over which they have little or no control. These events will cause blips in their returns and thus their d ratios.

As proof of this consistency, let's take the track records of the two managers of the Best and Random Funds we followed in the Chapter 5 section on fat tails. The Random Fund, which had a d ratio of 0.60, was a pro forma track record determined by $6^{1}/_{2}$ years of random monthly data. The Best Fund, which had a d ratio of 4.77, was a composite of the monthly returns of three of the largest and best-known macro hedge fund managers (Jaguar, Moore, and Tudor) during a $6^{1}/_{2}$-year time period from January 1990 to June 1996. Charts 8.1 and 8.2 show the manager's rolling d ratios within a ±1 standard deviation band.

Comparing Charts 8.1 and 8.2, we can see that our quarterly rolling d ratios are quite volatile over time for both managers.

CHART 8.1

Best manager quarterly rolling *d* ratio, January 1990 to June 1996.

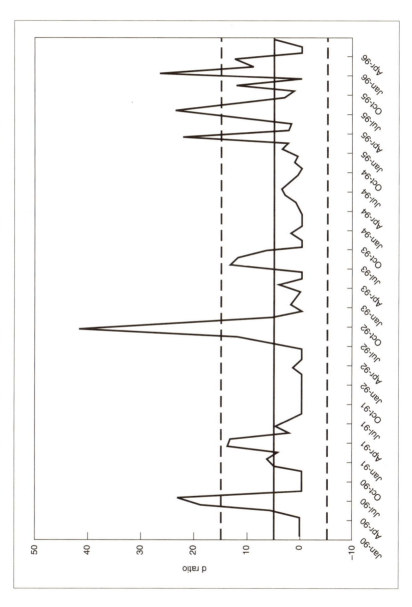

Source: Lara Capital.

CHART 8.2

Random manager quarterly rolling d ratio, January 1990 to June 1996.

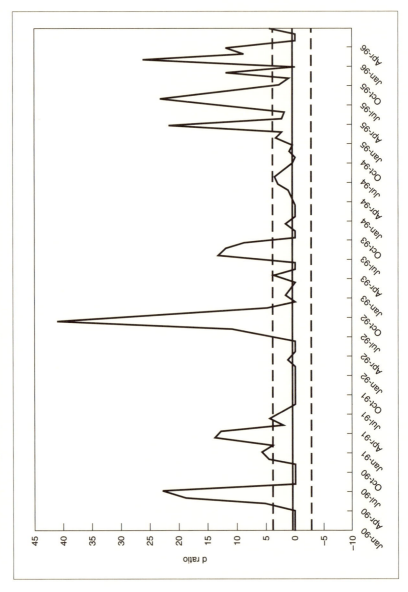

d ratio

Source: Lara Capital.

However, the rolling d ratio of our composite Best Fund manager is more predictable, falling for the most part within ±1 standard deviation range of its average value of 0.6 for the period as shown in Chart 8.1. This is clearly not the case with the Worse Fund, our synthetic skill-less manager. Chart 4.2 shows how this value is not only very unstable but also fluctuates well outside the ±1 standard deviation band of its long-term value of 4.77.

We believe that these two examples readily support the fact that skillful managers will tend to have more stable and predictable d ratios over time.

RANDOMNESS: LUCK, SKILL, AND BLACK BOXES

We've explained that luck is the result of the random patterns in a random market. We have also seen how this can be detected by analyzing the type and stability of a manager's skew over time. In this chapter we show how any manager who bases investment decisions on a random technique—the toss of a coin or a dartboard—will inevitably have returns that follow those of a random distribution, independently of the characteristic of the underlying market. To state this in another way, a manager who invests systematically in a random market will have random returns, as will a manager who invests randomly in a systematic market. This allows us to claim that rigid investment rules or systems such as black boxes or other technical trading systems can give rise to the same outside short-term gains, produced by luck, and which inevitably prove just as transitory. It is for this reason that investors, when they detect such managers, should give them the same wide berth they give "lucky" managers.

To clarify these points, let's look at three different hypothetical managers. Each of these managers invests with a clear system in the "market" outlined in Table 8.1.

- *Mr. Random.*   As a passive manager, he invests a dollar every month. If the market goes up, he makes a dollar.

If it goes down, he loses a dollar. Independently of whether he made or lost money the previous month, Mr. Random will always invest a new dollar the following month.

- *Mr. Martingale.* As a system-following manager, he invests a variable amount. He starts out by betting a dollar. If the market goes up, he makes a dollar, and reinvests a dollar the next month. If the market goes down, he loses a dollar, but in the following period invests twice the amount of his loss. Mr. Martingale's trading strategy is what professional traders call a "doubling up on loss" strategy.

- *Ms. Bidem.* As another system-following manager, she invests a variable amount. She starts out by betting a dollar. Every time she wins, she doubles her investment the next period. If she loses, she returns to betting a dollar the next period. Ms. Bidem's trading strategy is what professional traders call a "doubling up on gains" strategy.

These three managers present very distinct track records. Chart 8.3 shows the cumulative returns of these managers when we applied their strategy to the market illustrated in Table 8.1.

From Chart 8.3 it is tempting to conclude that the doubling-up strategies used by Mr. Martingale and Ms. Bidem are evidence of skill. After all, these managers substantially outperformed the market. However, that is an incorrect assumption. Each strategy outlined merely followed market events passively. The results they generated are ultimately attributable to the short-term behavior of the market and specifically how each strategy exploits the pattern of random runs. As it turns out, the random runs favored Mr. Martingale's strategy. Changes in the distributions of the runs in subsequent periods can and will alter the future success of his strategies and those of his fellow managers.

From these examples we can conclude that if the underlying market is random, rigid investment rules or systems may

CHART 8.3

Cumulative returns for Mr. Random, Mr. Martingale, and Ms. Bidem over the 60-day period market of Table 8.1.

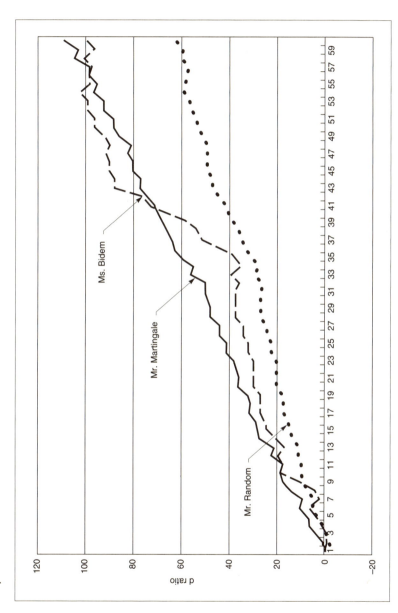

capture and enlarge short-term deviations in the market's odds. However, the market's true long-term odds must eventually reassert themselves. When this happens any short-term gains will disappear and any managers who were dependent on this luck for their performance will be forced to give back their gains.

As these examples show, if one has only a short track record to review and without more powerful analytical tools, it can be difficult to distinguish between a lucky and a skillful manager.

RANDOMNESS: DISTINGUISHING LUCK FROM SKILL

Let us return to our three managers, Mr. Random, Mr. Martingale, and Ms. Bidem again and see what more we can learn from analyzing their performance. We'll start by looking at the distribution of Mr. Random's returns.

As expected, Mr. Random's returns show a slight positive skew in line with the underlying market, confirmed by a d ratio of 7.4. His return can be approximated by a normal distribution as shown in Chart 8.4. What is more interesting is the instability of these returns as shown in Chart 8.5.

The wide volatility of Mr. Random's d ratio over the period in question confirms the instability of the manager's skew, namely, the lack of consistent skill being applied. This is especially clear if we notice how little of the rolling d ratio falls within the ±1-SD (standard deviation) band of the long-term d ratio. This allows us to conclude that Mr. Random brings us no value-added assets, either in absolute terms or relative to the market.

Let us now look at the distribution of Mr. Martingale's returns shown in Chart 8.6.

Despite Mr. Martingale's investment success, illustrated in Chart 8.1 and the positive skew confirmed by a d ratio of 16.8, it is surprising to discover that Mr. Martingale's returns can be approximated by a normal distribution. Chart 8.6 illustrates this point clearly. It also confirms our statement that managers

CHART   8.4

Distribution of Mr. Random's returns.

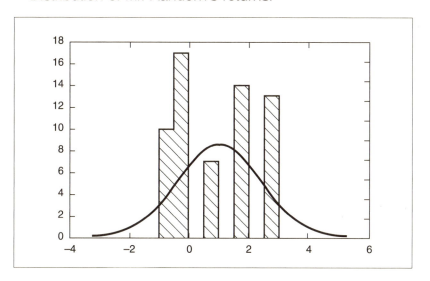

who do not apply skill in managing investments will have distributions that follow those of the underlying market. The random source and nature of Mr. Martingale's returns is confirmed by the nature and magnitude of the instability of his d ratio shown in Chart 8.6. Once again, we note how infrequently the rolling d ratios lie within the ±1-SD band of the long-term value of 16.87.

This wide discrepancy in Mr. Martingale's d-ratio values (see Chart 8.7) is particularly interesting, as it could be an indication that Mr. Martingale may soon underperform in future periods. As any trader knows, in a falling market the doubling up strategy is a sure recipe for disaster, and in the case of Mr. Martingale a short succession of down periods can quickly erode his gains.

Thus, despite his excellent performance to date, we can conclude that Mr. Martingale's performance may be unsustainable in the future, and that we are better off as investors in not allocating money to Mr. Martingale.

CHART 8.5

Changes in the value of Mr. Random's d ratio.

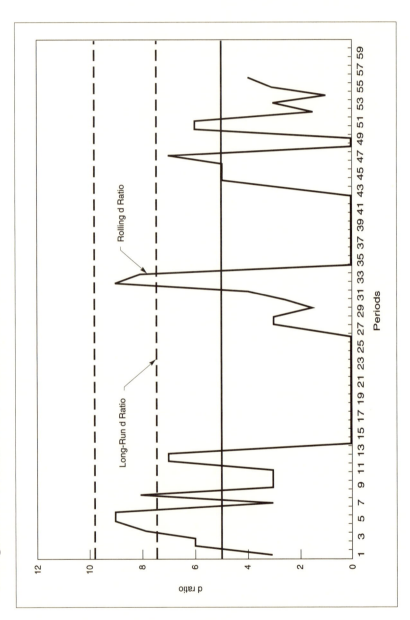

C H A R T   8.6

Distribution of Mr. Martingale's returns.

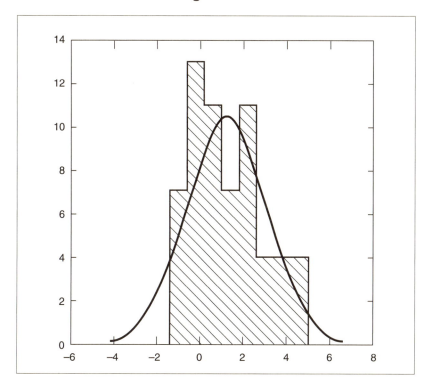

Finally, we'll review the distribution of Ms. Bidem's returns (see Chart 8.8).

An analysis of Ms. Bidem's results provides us with the same type of information we obtained from our analysis of Mr. Martingale's results. Because no true skill is applied by Ms. Bidem, the distribution of her returns can be approximated by a normal distribution, despite a negative skew of the returns and an unusual positive tail which give the distribution a shape substantially different from Mr. Martingale's. These unusual characteristics are confirmed by a d ratio lower than those of the other managers: 5.6. Clearly this difference is caused by the different nature of Ms. Bidem's rule-based strategy.

CHART 8.7

Changes in the value of Mr. Martingale's d ratio.

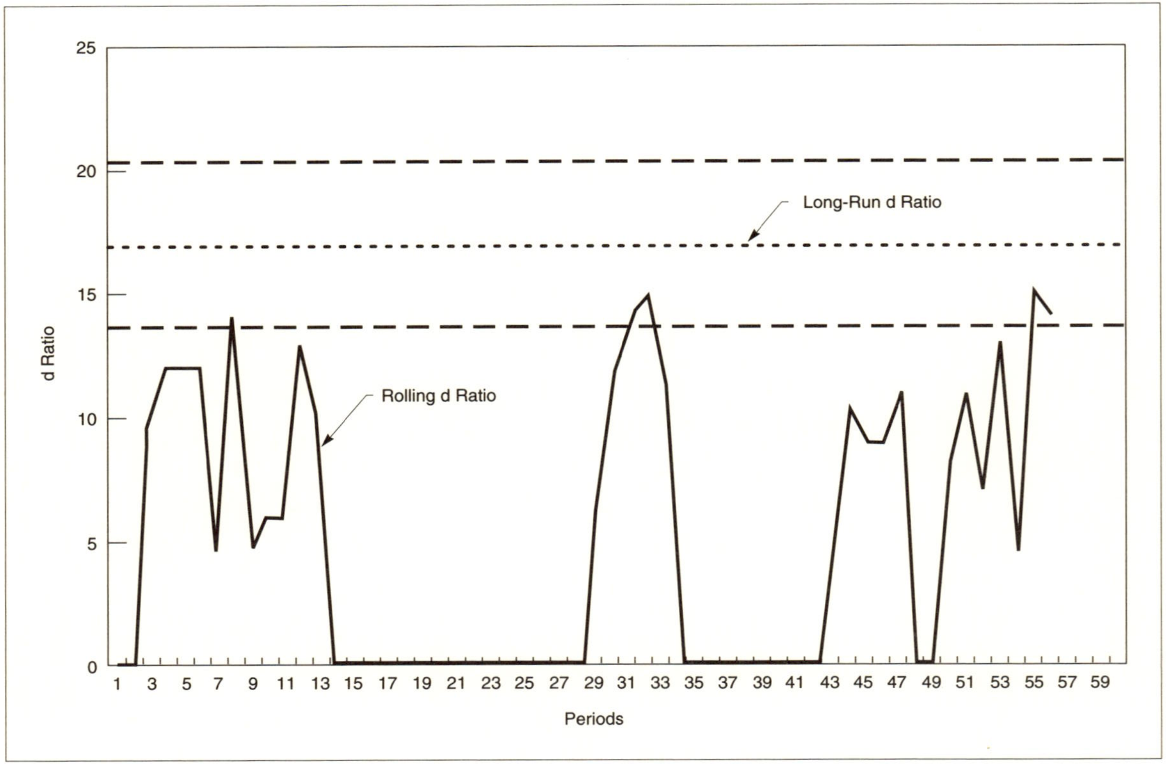

CHART 8.8

Distribution of Ms. Bidem's returns.

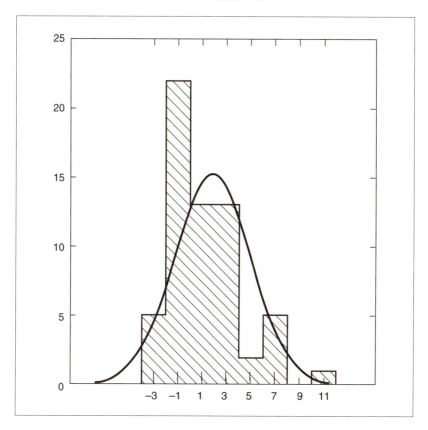

Nonetheless, the conformity of Ms. Bidem's returns to a normal distribution confirms the presence of randomness. If we focus our attention on the rolling d ratio, we see its extreme instability, shown in Chart 8.9. Note the limited number of values which fall within ±1-SD band.

From this analysis we can conclude that although future random runs may aid Ms. Bidem's strategy, she remains a risky investment. As investors, we would do well to steer clear of her.

In these three cases we can see that by studying the conformity of a manager's returns to a normal distribution and

CHART 8.9

Changes in the value of Ms. Bidem's d ratio.

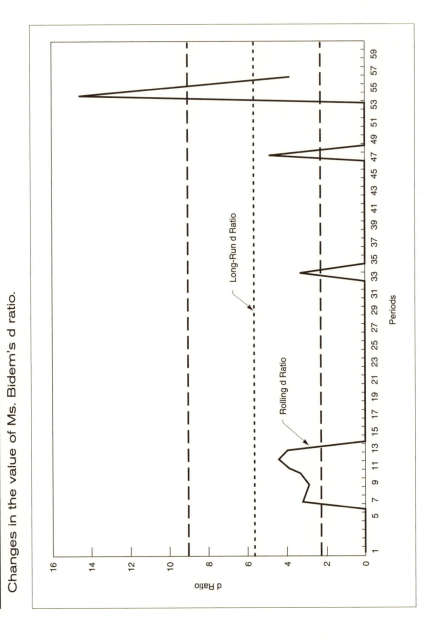

the stability of their d ratios, we can make informed judgments on whether a manager's returns were caused by luck or skill. We can also see how passive investment strategies such as doubling up on losses or pyramiding gains can give the appearance of investment skill, without giving any value-added to an investor. These passive strategies will also influence the distribution of a manager's returns and the absolute level of that manager's long-term d ratio. Despite these potential distortions, an analysis of the short-term rolling d ratios will appear highly unstable and warn us of the lack of true skill.

RANDOMNESS AND RISK IN HEDGE FUNDS

So far we have seen that the defining characteristic of hedge funds is the managers' skills and their abilities to consistently pick winners, identify market inefficiencies, let their winners run, and cut their own losses. Furthermore, all this must be done in a consistent and systematic manner to obtain above-average returns with less than incremental risk. This means that each manager must not only have developed a distinct personal investment approach or set of rules but also follow and apply these rules consistently. For this approach to bear fruit, it is also necessary for the market in which the manager is operating to favor this approach or set of rules.

A manager's success is thus determined by the favorable combination of two elements: the market and that manager's approach. Managers who can consistently combine these elements in their favor will achieve two things: d ratios that are very stable over time, and the ability to provide their investors with considerable value-added. Managers who are not skillful will have d ratios that fluctuate in a random fashion.

As investors, deviations in the d ratio, either from historical values or in absolute terms, indicate that the manager's skill may be nonexistent or eroding. However, as an indication for monitoring managers, the d ratio alone gives us only a partial picture, since it is a backward-looking statistic. In monitoring managers we need additional information to determine whether any changes in a particular manager's d ratio are the result of temporary fluctuations, or represent a departure from the norm and signal a red flag on the safety of our investment.

CHAPTER 9

Identifying Hedge Fund Manager Skills

MANAGER SKILLS: INTERPRETING d-RATIO CHANGES

Analyzing how a manager's d ratio changes over time allows us to gain insights into the permanence of a manager's skill. It is invaluable in evaluating the value-added that a manager could bring to our portfolio. However, it is a backward-looking tool. After we have made our allocation, monitoring a manager through changes in the d ratio is ineffective. The changes we may see from time to time tell us little of any value until it is too late for us to protect our investment. To monitor managers, we need to find some way of knowing if fluctuations in their returns (and thus their d ratios) are temporary or permanent, and whether we should be concerned about a particular manager continuing to bring us value-added. This kind of information would allow us to make informed decisions about when to reposition our investment with a manager.

MANAGER SKILLS: IDENTIFYING REVERSION TO MEAN

The easiest way to verify if changes in a manager's d ratio are transitory is to see if it is mean-reverting. In other words, if we can expect changes in the d ratio value to be reversed and converge toward a predictable long-term value. We can expect that managers with mean-reverting d ratios are attractive for us as investors, since they give us a high possibility of producing constant value-added.

One way to identify mean reversion is through the *Hurst index*,[1] which expresses numerically the tendency for a manager's track record to fluctuate around a certain average value, without making any assumptions about the behavior of the underlying variables.

By telling us the nature of a manager's fluctuation around a mean, the Hurst index, which can assume values between 0 and 1, allows us to determine if the manager's performance is random, persistent, or mean-reverting. This allows us to derive impressions about a manager's performance that may be used to make effective decisions on the safety and effectiveness of our investment.

To understand this point better, let's look at the different values the Hurst index can assume. Specifically, if the index falls within the following ranges:

- *Between 0 and 0.5* we can consider a manager's track record as antipersistent. This means the manager's returns will tend to fluctuate randomly, but over time tend to converge to a stable value. While generating variable results, such a manager will produce long-term results over time for us, assuming that the long-term values towards which these results will converge are greater than zero.
- *Around 0.5* we can consider a manager's track record as totally random. This means that we can expect that the manager's returns in one period are not influenced by those of previous periods. A manager such as this should be avoided, for reasons we'll see further on.

---

[1] For a discussion of the Hurst index and how it may be derived from hedge fund track record funds, please refer to App. 4.

■ *Between 0.5 and 1* we can consider the manager's track record as persistent. This means that we can expect the managers in any one period to be strongly influenced by those of previous periods. To our knowledge, no managers have consistently persistent returns for long periods of time. Such managers, at least in theory, would be a modern equivalent of King Midas, turning everything they touch to gold. For this reason encountering a manager's track record with such characteristics should be taken with a healthy degree of skepticism.

MANAGER SKILLS: HURST INDICES AND HEDGE FUND MANAGERS

As it turns out, most successful hedge fund managers have Hurst indices, which, for the most part, show mean-reverting behavior. In all fairness it would seem that some hedge fund types have Hurst indices that are uncomfortably close to the 0.5 random value for the index. Table 9.1 illustrates these findings by showing the values of the Hurst index for all the major hedge fund types, and contrasting them with the applicable standard deviation statistics.

It is also interesting to note in Table 9.1 that as the degree of directionality in a hedge fund's style increases, so does the degree with which its Hurst index converges toward 0.5.

Stated another way, Table 9.1 tells us that the less market directionality in a manager's style, the greater the certainty we can have in predicting that this manager's returns will converge to a known value. If the manager's returns are above average for one month, then there is a good probability that they will be below average the next month, and vice versa. This ensures that over time we will see both a fairly permanent and consistent average value for the manager's returns. As investors, this means constant value-added. However, long-term Hurst indices derived from all of a manager's track record

TABLE 9.1

Hurst Index Values and Standard Deviation for Major
Hedge Fund Groupings, January 1994 to December
1998

Hedge Fund Style	Long-Term Hurst Index	Standard Deviation, %
Macro	0.331585	3.35
Market timing	0.345564	3.57
Equity hedge	0.416839	4.60
Convertible arbitrage	0.419554	2.93
Emerging markets	0.443483	3.17
Market-neutral	0.453115	3.86
Merger	0.475154	4.49
Event-driven	0.477709	3.87
Distressed	0.479532	4.39
Relative value	0.480771	3.64
Mortgage	0.494584	4.30

Source: Hfr and Lara Capital.

are of limited value, as we showed for other statistics earlier in this book.

The value of a Hurst index is ultimately determined by the dynamics of the manager's investment style and the markets. Thus, we can expect values of the Hurst index to be variable, calculated using a rolling-window technique. It is hardly surprising to discover that the short-term values of the Hurst index derived from a rolling-window technique can tell us much more about a manager. As it turns out, they are singularly useful in monitoring a manager's performance after we have made our investment.

MANAGER SKILLS: HURST INDICES AND MANAGER EVALUATIONS

To understand what short-term changes in a Hurst index can tell about a manager, let us take two extreme cases from Table

9.1. In particular, let's focus on the hedge fund styles that exhibited the highest and lowest Hurst indices: macro and the mortgage managers. In Charts 9.1 and 9.2 we plot the changes in the rolling annual Hurst indices for these two hedge fund styles and compare them to the long-term values we derived for Table 9.1.

Unsurprisingly, the volatility of the rolling Hurst indices in Charts 9.1 and 9.2 is directly related to the value of the absolute value of the Hurst index shown in Table 9.1. Mortgage hedge fund managers show greater volatility in their rolling Hurst index than do macro hedge fund managers. However, in Charts 9.2 and 9.3 there is another issue, which is more interesting to explore. From these charts we notice that the short-term rolling Hurst indices assume values which can be random, persistent, or antipersistent. Do these shorter-term values allow us to determine any information about a manager's behavior? To answer this question, let us look at how the Hurst index fluctuates within a 1-SD band of its long-term value, and contrast this with the monthly return numbers for the index. Chart 9.3 shows the results of this analysis on macro hedge fund managers, while Chart 9.4 shows our results for mortgage fund managers.

Let us start by inspecting macro hedge fund managers in Chart 9.3. One of the first things we notice is that, on average, extreme changes in monthly performance appear to be associated with deviations in excess of a 1 percent standard deviation of the long-term Hurst index. Stated in another way, whenever short-term Hurst indices deviate from the 1-SD band, the manager's monthly returns will experience a change whose size and direction will ensure that the manager's performance reverts to a predictable, mean value. However, looking more closely, we notice that at certain points in time the short-term Hurst index assumes values that are persistent (i.e., between 0.5 and 1). Whenever this happens, the manager's returns for the next period will be in the same direction as in the previous periods before reverting. The same type of behavior holds true

CHART 9.1

Macro hedge fund manager index: rolling 12-month Hurst index versus long-term index value, January 1994 to December 1998.

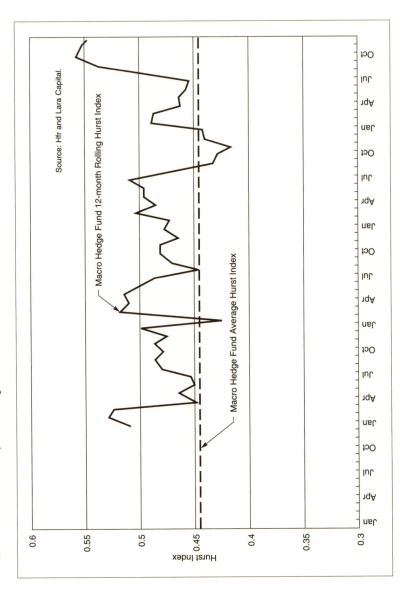

Source: Hfr and Lara Capital.

Macro Hedge Fund 12-month Rolling Hurst Index

Macro Hedge Fund Average Hurst Index

Hurst Index

CHART 9.2

Mortgage hedge fund manager index: rolling 12-month Hurst index versus long-term index value, January 1994 to December 1998.

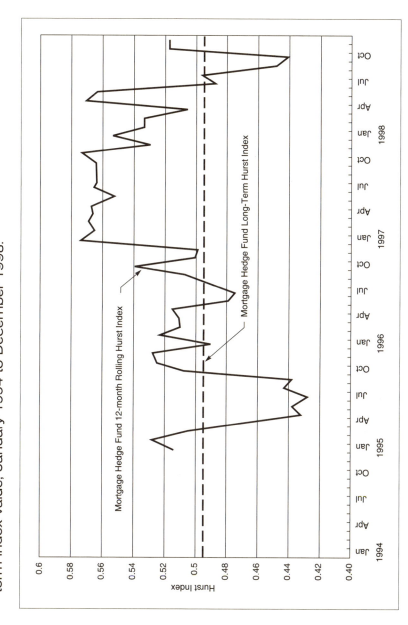

CHART 9.3

Macro hedge fund manager monthly returns versus Hurst index in a 1-SD band, January 1994 to December 1998.

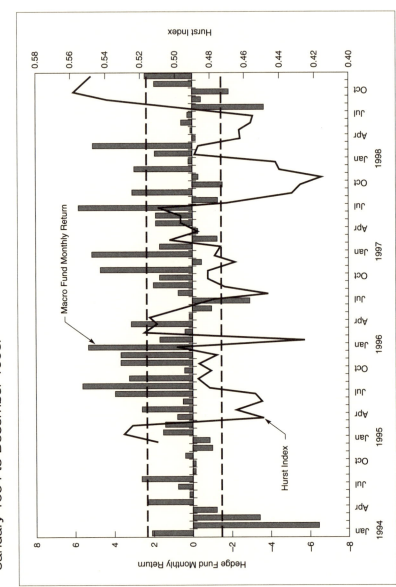

Source: Hfr and Lara Capital.

CHART 9.4

Mortgage hedge fund manager monthly returns versus Hurst index in a 1-SD band, January 1994 to December 1998.

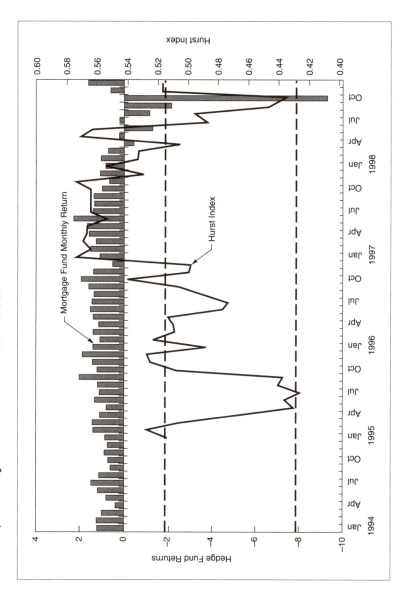

Source: Hfr and Lara Capital.

113

when the short-term Hurst index assumes antipersistent values (i.e., between 0 and 0.5). In this case the manager's returns reverse, directly in the following period. It would seem that changes in the value of the Hurst index allow us to form some expectation as to the direction, speed, and size of a manager's performance from one period to the next. Using this insight allows us to monitor a manager's performance in an effective manner.

To confirm the validity of such an insight let's look at the behavior of our mortgage manager index. From Table 9.1 we saw these hedge funds had a Hurst index close to 0.5, and had a wide standard deviation attached to this number. From this we concluded that the group's returns should be fairly random, but we should also see wide swings in the value of the short-term Hurst index.

Inspecting Chart 9.4, one of the first things we notice is the high volatility of the short-term Hurst index. The Hurst index goes from having substantially mean-reverting values (less than 0.5) to substantially persistent ones (greater than 0.5). In particular, we note that for periods when the index has persistent values, we have consecutive periods of monthly gains, followed by sudden violent corrections, when the Hurst index changes direction and begins to assume random or antipersistent values. As we saw in our discussion of luck, such behavior is very consistent with random runs on a manager's performance. It is hardly surprising that the long-term value of the Hurst index for mortgage managers should be so close to the random value of 0.5.

From our discussion in this chapter, it is clear that the Hurst index is a powerful tool that can be used in a variety of ways. In a historical context it can be used to highlight and validate impressions we may have formed about a manager from other sources or statistics. In an ongoing context it can be used to monitor a manager's behavior to highlight potential problems, and so ensure the safety of our investment.

Our discussion of the Hurst index also highlighted, once again, the issue of randomness in a manager's returns. This time it did so without having made any assumptions about the underlying distribution. Given the way randomness continues to appear in our analysis, perhaps it is time to explore any further implications it could have on our wealth, which may give us further insights into hedge funds and their operations.

CHAPTER 10

Randomness and Hedge Fund Failure

RANDOMNESS: GAMBLER'S RUIN, OR WHY HEDGE FUNDS GO BUST

Intuitively we have formed the impression that randomness in a manager's returns is a precursor to losses. To explain why, and gain insight about what impact this could have for us as investors, we need to use some of the fruits of mathematical research into randomness, probability, and activities such as gambling, where money can be earned from the outcome of uncertain or random events.

From a mathematical perspective, investing and speculating share many of the same traits (no moral judgment implied here); it is relatively easy to apply much of this research to investing and, by extension, to hedge funds and their activities. Unfortunately, most of this work is abstract, highly mathematical, and often counterintuitive. A detailed treatment of the subject requires heavy proofs and advanced differential calculus. For this reason we will avoid excessive detail, limiting ourselves to extracting and presenting, in the most simplified manner possible, the tools and formulas needed to make our case, using convenient approximations of the underlying functions for the sake of simplicity.[1] We recognize that the substantial simplifications we will make will detract from the rigor of our case. At the same time, they will considerably increase the readability of these chapters and the points we are trying to make. For this reason, we beg the indulgence of the more mathematically inclined readers.

One of the most interesting tools for highlighting the perils of randomness is the "gambler's ruin" paradigm. The most basic principle of this paradigm is that managers facing even odds of making money in a random market, such as Mr. Random in Chap. 8, will lose all their investors' money. The exact probability with which this will occur is determined by the amount of leverage used by a manager. In other words, in a random market with even odds of winning, a manager who uses more leverage has a greater chance of going bust. For the readers who suffered through our discussion of leverage in Chap. 7, there is nothing surprising about this conclusion. However, what may be surprising is the nonlinear nature of this relationship as illustrated in Chart 10.1.

To understand why, let's use a basic formulation of the gambler's-ruin paradigm. It states that in the special case of even odds (i.e., a 50 percent chance of winning or losing money), the probability Q of the manager losing all the fund's money can be approximated by the following formula:

$$Q = 1 - \frac{K}{B} \qquad (10.1)$$

where K is the notional value of the manager's positions and B represents the hedge fund's capital.

As we can see in Chart 10.1, when leverage exceeds 9:1, the probability of a manager losing an investor's capital rapidly converges to 100 percent. Conversely, for no leverage, the possibility of a manager losing all an investor's

---

[1] Interested readers are referred to the Bibliography, where sources containing more detailed discussions of these topics are listed.

CHART 10.1

The nonlinear nature of leverage and the probability of loss under the gambler's-ruin paradigm.

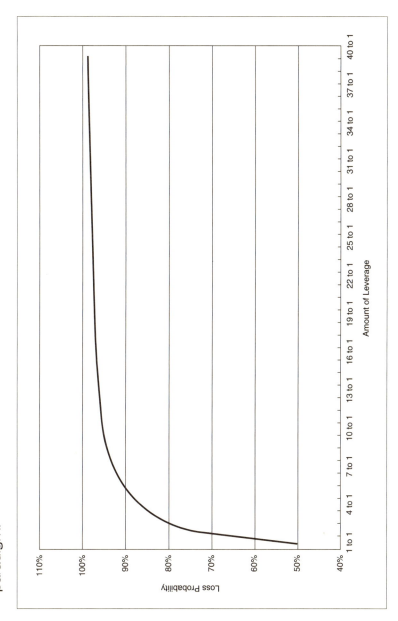

money is determined by the underlying odds of the market: 50 percent.

By using the gambler's-ruin paradigm we can also determine how quickly a manager will lose an investor's money. Once again, the duration of the fund D is a function of the amount of leverage used. It can be approximated by the following formula:

$$D = K^*(B - K) \qquad (10.2)$$

where D = the duration of the manager's fund (in this case, expressed in years)

B = the notional value of the manager's positions

K = the size of the fund's capital

Assuming that the positions are revalued hourly, Eq. (10.2) tells us that a manager with U.S. $100,000,000 under management and who used leverage of 3:1 can, with a probability of 67 percent, be expected to lose all an investor's money in 2.31 years! This is not a particularly exciting prospect for an investor, especially as it will be if confirmed later from other actual and theoretical data.

In Chap. 8 we discussed how random runs might cause a hedge fund manager to outperform the market for short periods of time. It is therefore fair to ask what the odds are of a hedge fund manager having a winning streak during the 2.31 years of a fund's expected life. The answer is, very good.

We can approximate this probability, using some of the mathematical properties that mathematicians and physicists ascribe to particles which move about in a random fashion, called *brownian motion*. These properties of brownian motion are called the *arc-sine law,* and are used to understand and model the behavior of things such as water molecules in boiling water or dust motes (small particles) in the air. For our purposes we will use a special case of the *arc-sine law,*[2] which

---

[2] We can express this law as $F \sim \dfrac{1}{\Pi_i^n \cdot \sqrt{c(c - t)}}$, where F represents the probability of a continuous win of length $2t$ and t is the period of expected wins, n is the number of expected wins.

allows us to derive, under the assumption of even odds, that a manager has a 27 percent probability of generating a 6-month period of continuous wins before going bust in 2.31 years. A year of continuous wins, under the same assumption, has a probability of around 24 percent. Thus the manager will almost certainly lose all an investor's money in 2.31 years but is almost 30 percent likely to generate superior performance for over one-third (36 percent, to be precise) of the fund's life!

Some readers may find the reasoning on this point esoteric, but if they pause to reflect, these conclusions go a long way toward explaining the phenomenon of "hot" managers in the real world. The performance of these managers often seems comparable to that of shooting stars, shining very briefly before burning themselves out and disappearing from view. As savvy investors, we would like to avoid the transitory charms of these types of managers, given the negative impact they inevitably have on our wealth.

Our efforts in Chap. 8 to determine managers with a high degree of randomness in their returns now pay off, as they allow us to detect and avoid such shooting stars. As the various arguments we made in this book on skill, randomness, and consistent performance fall together, we see how managers with a high element of randomness in their returns, no matter how stellar their short-term performance, eventually have a very high probability of losing their investors' money.

Practical readers will note that the wide, sweeping results and impressive generalizations we have made so far appear to rest on a very fragile assumption. This assumption is that managers operate in markets where they face even odds of making money. What happens if this is not the case?

We have already explored how dynamic trading strategies, risk control, leverage, and the ability to identify investments with attractive risks and rewards can allow truly skillful hedge fund managers to generate favorable odds, possibly ad infinitum. As we saw in Chaps. 5 and 9, this skill was evidenced by the skew of the distribution of a manager's returns and the relative stability of this distribution over time. For such managers the strictures of permanently skewed returns clearly do not apply. Unfortunately, the complexities of the math describing the managers do not allow us to make the easy generalizations and predictions of Eqs. (10.1) and (10.2). The only thing we can say with any certainty is that managers who face attractive odds *can* boost their returns with leverage, without increasing risks. Furthermore, because they have no clear limits on their performance, they can theoretically continue their activities indefinitely.

On the other hand, hedge fund managers often face unfavorable odds. Factors such as imperfect information, transaction costs, execution slippage, and other handicaps of real-world investing can do much to stack the odds against a manager. These factors can also erode an edge that the manager may have developed or exhibited earlier but cannot maintain for any number of reasons. Theoretically, a rational hedge fund manager facing unfavorable odds should not raise money from clients or continue to invest. From time to time some hedge fund managers have returned money to their investors and liquidated their funds when they felt they were losing their edge. Such cases are, unfortunately, the exception rather than the norm in the world of hedge funds. Often, greed, hubris, and ignorance go a long way toward blinding hedge fund managers to poor or slipping skills (and thus to maintaining favorable odds over the market).

In all fairness, not all managers are so cynical. Many hedge funds in their start-up phase knowingly face unfavorable odds, which may be overcome when the fund reaches optimal size. In these cases the need to generate attractive returns both to bootstrap the fund's size and generate fees, forces managers to accept this challenge. In such circumstances, the optimal behavior for such managers can once again be suggested by the mathematical treatment of the games of chance. Mathematicians have shown that facing unfavorable odds, the only way for managers to generate the greatest returns for their investors is to adopt the strategy of maximum avarice, or what is known as the "greedy algorithm," possibly one of the most counterintuitive products of this research.

In the present context this means the best chance a start-up fund has of generating attractive returns is to make a large bet—the bigger, the better! Similarly, managers whose skills are slipping can bolster their performance by concentrating their positions. In the case of a one-bet strategy, we can approximate the odds of winning G by means of the following formula:

$$G = \frac{(R{\cdot}K - 1)}{(R{\cdot}B - 1)} \tag{10.3}$$

when RK is the size of the manager's positions at risk as a percentage of the fund's capital and RB represents the notional size of the manager's position as a percentage of the notional size of the capital.

In Eq. (10.3), the difference between the actual size and the notional size of the positions and the capital is given by the amount of leverage employed by the manager.

Chart 10.2 plots the probability of a hedge fund manager maximizing the fund's returns under different bet sizes and leverage scenarios. This chart was derived using Eq. (10.3), and assumes that the manager faces a market with only a 40 percent chance of winning. As this illustration shows, the larger the bet and the better the leverage, the greater possibility that the manager will maximize the fund's returns. In this specific case, leverage can quickly generate a situation of highly probable, high returns by allowing the manager to increase the size of the bet well in excess of available capital. The downside is, of course, a higher chance of mortality, if the bet has an unfavorable outcome.

The scenario so far has assumed a one-bet game with constant probabilities at each bet. In the real world, managing a fund can be considered similar to placing a series of bets over time (basically, one for each period the fund is marked to market), with changing odds. The more one (viz., the manager) wins, the more money one can place at risk the next period,

CHART 10.2

Importance of bet size (expressed as percentage of the fund's capital) in maximizing returns under unfavorable odds.

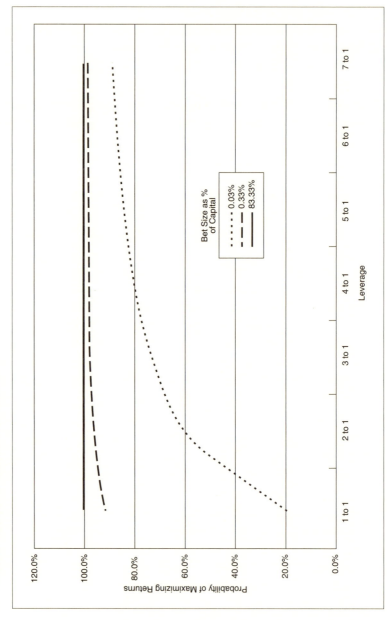

Bet Size as %
of Capital

.... 0.03%
— — — 0.33%
———— 83.33%

Leverage

Probability of Maximizing Returns

either on the same positions or on a new one, if one has not lost everything as the result of an unfavorable outcome. As it turns out, even in a multibet strategy with variable odds, betting everything is an optimal strategy. The explanation is much harder to illustrate in a similar intuitive manner. The total probability of winning is a nonlinear self-recursive function, with the odds of winning in each period given by the gains in the previous one. This function is incredibly difficult to compute with precision.[3] However, once again the downside to maximizing returns with a greedy strategy is a shortened expected life span for the fund. As time passes, the odds of losing everything increase dramatically, as shown in Chart 10.3.

Chart 10.3 shows that, on the basis of the greedy algorithm, the amount of time during which a manager can successfully apply an investment strategy is finite. The more the leverage used to maximize returns, the shorter the expected life span of the fund. To get an idea as to how long this could be, we can use the approximation shown in the following formula, provided we assume a constant size of the positions at risk:

$$D = \frac{1}{P \cdot (R - 1) \cdot [K - B] \cdot X} \tag{10.4}$$

where D = expected duration of investment fund
P = market odds in manager's favor
$R = (1 - P)/P$
K = fund's capital
B = notional value of the fund's positions
$X = K/B$

By applying Eq. (10.4) to a U.S. \$300,000,000 fund, we can derive a series of possible expected lives for a fund, assuming hourly reevaluations, leverage scenarios ranging from 1:1 to 7:1, and different market odds for the manager from 60 to 20

---

[3] Assuming n investment periods, this probability W can be approximated by $W(n) = p^n(p + 2q)$, where p is the manager's odds of winning and q is $1 - p$, with $0 < p < 0.5$.

CHART 10.3

Success in multiperiod greedy strategies comes at the expense of higher mortality rates.

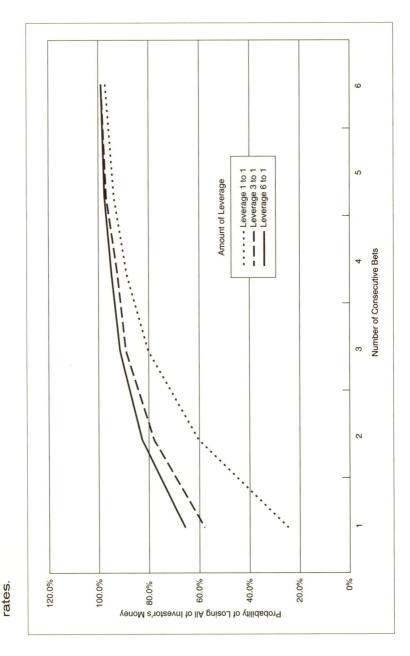

percent. We have plotted the outcomes of these simulations as a pie chart in Chart 10.4.

Looking at Chart 10.4, we can see that there is an 83.34 percent chance that the fund will have a life span of 4.5 years or less and a 47.62 percent chance that its life span will be between 1.4 and 4.5 years. These numbers are remarkably close to the estimates we obtained earlier, even having allowed for more realistic assumptions in terms of market odds and leverage. Despite the highly abstract conditions under which these numbers were generated, the theory seems to be telling us that hedge funds should experience very high mortality rates. Specifically, the theory tells us that within 4.5 years of their launch, over 80 percent of all new hedge funds will go out of business because they will have lost their investors' money. Clearly, if such high mortality rates exist in the real world, hedge fund investing should be treated with extreme caution and care.

RANDOMNESS: HEDGE FUND MORTALITY RATES

It is hard to determine hedge fund mortality rates precisely because of the lack of reliable hedge fund data. This is unfortunate, given the implications of mortality in the evaluation of hedge funds (the so-called survivor bias).

Few of the existing commercial databases containing hedge fund information keep track of, or distinguish between, hedge funds that have gone out of business and those that no longer report to the database vendor. There are many reasons for this. A common example we have encountered is that of a *closing fund:* a hedge fund which, having reached its target asset size, may choose to no longer report to the database as marketing reasons no longer drive the managers' need to disseminate data to the public via the database. Such managers will disappear from a hedge fund database, while continuing to operate profitably. More information is required to be able to use database information as a source for hedge fund mortality rates.

Fortunately, we have been able to research and gather a reliable 10-year database of 901 funds operated by 546 different

CHART 10.4

Distribution of hedge fund's expected life under leverage ranges from 1:1 to 7:1 and market odds from 60 to 20 percent in the managers' favor.

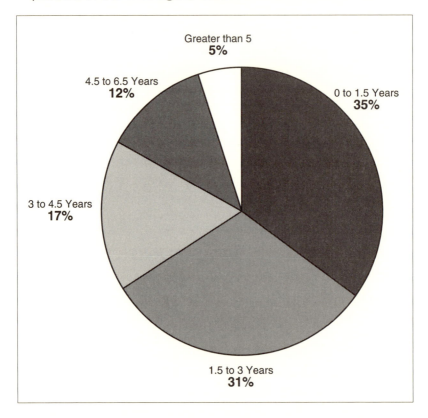

Greater than 5
5%

4.5 to 6.5 Years
12%

0 to 1.5 Years
35%

3 to 4.5 Years
17%

1.5 to 3 Years
31%

managers. Since 1988, when we first started collecting the data, 304 funds operated by 191 managers remain in operation. On the other hand, 597 funds have been dissolved and 355 managers have gone out of business. These figures give us a staggering mortality rate of over 66 percent. Of the funds and managers that closed, the average life span was about 3.5 years,[4] roughly consistent with the expectation we had formed in the preceding section.

---

[4] These data are confirmed by research by the Milken Foundation and by Tass Management, an information database vendor.

CHAPTER 11

Hedge Funds and Portfolio Allocation

HEDGE FUND PORTFOLIO ALLOCATION: NONLINEAR HEDGE FUND RETURNS

In Chap. 10 we saw how the use of leverage makes hedge fund risks and returns behave in a manner that is highly nonlinear, and in many ways highly fractal in nature. (*Note:* Fractal is a mathematical term used to describe a process self similar in nature, i.e., one that appears to look the same if we were to zoom in or out of a graphical representation of this process.) Unfortunately, these characteristics make hedge funds difficult to represent mathematically and warp the usefulness of many of the traditional statistical tools used to evaluate them. Traditional tools may, as we saw previously, cause investors to make incorrect evaluations and do not need to be explored again here.

In this chapter we want to review another area where the peculiar behavior of hedge funds can have a significant and misunderstood effect on investors. This is the use of hedge funds in portfolio allocation, and the creation of funds.

HEDGE FUND PORTFOLIO ALLOCATION: THE NEED TO PROCEED WITH CAUTION

In a world of traditional assets—stocks, bonds, commodities, or mutual funds—knowing the asset's average returns, its standard deviation, and its correlation to the other assets in the portfolio made asset allocation easy. We could use canned software based on well-known and academically established methods to compute an ideal, risk-effective portfolio. The resulting combination of funds and assets was a portfolio that allowed us to maximize our returns while reducing our over-all risk. Furthermore, we could have a relatively high degree of confidence in how the resulting allocation worked. However, this process rests on the assumption that the num-bers for the average returns, standard deviations, and correla-tion numbers are meaningful and realistic. In other words, the average returns really are average returns, standard devia-tions really computed our risks, and the correlation among our assets actually represented the way the value of our assets moved together.

Alas, with hedge funds we can have no such certainties. In Chap. 5 we described how the skill of a hedge fund man-ager could skew the distribution of the fund's returns, throw-ing off return and risk estimates based on means and standard deviation. Furthermore, the speed and manner in which hedge funds can change their risk books influences their cor-relation, and thus their apparent exposure to asset classes. This affects the meaningfulness of the correlation statistic as a diversification tool. Taken together, such factors point to the perils of slavishly using traditional methods to construct port-folios containing hedge funds; also, it emerges that in the case of hedge funds, traditional approaches to portfolio allocation should be taken with a small truckload of salt. Hedge funds, particularly new ones, also present investors with two addi-tional complications when being considered for asset alloca-tion: survivor bias and asset concentration.

Survivor Bias

Chapter 10 pointed out that approximately two out of three hedge fund managers disappear from their maiden trade within 2 to 3 years. In light of these high mortality rates, hedge fund returns, especially new ones, will tend to understate the actual returns available to investors. Table 11.1 illustrates this point by showing the different return scenarios an investor faces when making a 4-year investment in a fund in which there is a 75 percent chance of sustaining a 40 percent loss in 4 years.

Table 11.1 shows why the returns investors should use in their asset allocations should be the lower effective risk-adjusted return (0.10 percent), not the historical average return of 15 percent per annum. Using higher unadjusted returns will overstate the yield pickup that hedge funds can give to an investor's portfolios and thus cause a heavier portfolio weighting than warranted. Clearly the example outlined in Table 11.1 is extreme, but our research using real-world hedge fund data in different portfolio allocation scenarios reveals that this overweighting factor can be as much as 20 percent.

TABLE 11.1

Actual and Effective Returns (in Percent per Annum) in a 4-Year Scenario with a 75 Percent Chance of a 40 Percent Bias in 4 Years

Years of Life	No Losses	Loss in Year 4	Loss in Year 3	Loss in Year 2
1	15.00	15.00	15.00	15.00
2	15.00	15.00	15.00	−40.00
3	15.00	15.00	−40.00	—
4	15.00	−40.00	—	—
Average return	15.00	1.25	−3.33	−12.50
Expected risk-adjusted return	0.10	—	—	—

Position Concentration

As explained in the hedge fund survival strategies discussed in Chap. 10, it makes sense for new hedge funds, or those suffering from declining manager skills, to concentrate their positions. This allows them to maximize returns in the face of unfavorable odds. For us as investors, this concentration of positions means that there is a greater chance of positions or exposures being repeated across different hedge fund styles. The benefits of diversification to an investor are effectively reduced by position concentration between different hedge funds. This is particularly worrisome, as it may be hard for investors to detect concentration, given the unreliability of the correlation numbers between actively managed funds, as we saw in Chap. 3. Traditional correlation-based diversification will not be effective more than 70 percent of the time, when hedge funds are included in a portfolio.

HEDGE FUND PORTFOLIO ALLOCATION: THE BENEFITS OF CAUTION

Our firm has done much research into the potential benefits of rethinking the ways and the methods used to add hedge funds to investor's portfolios. Our research has found that traditional approaches tend to overdiversify an investor's portfolios among hedge funds. Worse, because of the unreliability of the correlation number used, traditional algorithms tend to cause pseudodiversification by splitting an investor's portfolio between funds that ultimately have the same risk sensitivity.

Adjusting for such factors, we have found that effective portfolios that mix assets and mutual funds can usually be achieved with *half* the number of hedge funds and assets computed by a traditional portfolio allocation model. At the same time the resulting portfolio generally had 50 percent higher returns, with 25 percent less risk (as measured by negative volatility). While the exact mechanics of how these results are achieved depend on proprietary techniques developed and owned by Lara Capital, Inc., the explanation of these surprising and powerful results can be explained intuitively. In our discussion of greedy algorithms we emphasized how funds with concentrated positions tend to have better odds of surviving and better performance over the short term. At the same time, in today's global financial markets there are few attractive trends or market opportunities for a hedge fund to exploit during the course of a year. This means that, taken as a whole, many hedge funds tend to have similar or closely related positions in their portfolios, at times independently of their professed investment mandate. Because of the similarity of their positions, the majority of hedge funds will have results that are closely correlated in down markets, but possibly weakly correlated in up markets. This is due in part to the way risk book structure can influence correlation. In such circumstances, because of biases in the return and correlation numbers, our portfolio allocation will contain too many hedge funds. In such a portfolio we are, in effect, reducing our upside (we are averaging it between more funds) without increasing our risk diversification in a down market.

HEDGE FUND PORTFOLIO ALLOCATION: INTEREST RATE SENSITIVITY

Given what we know so far about hedge funds, their operations, and the caution needed to add them effectively to a portfolio, there is one additional factor to which we should pay particular attention: their extreme sensitivity to interest rates. As we saw, leverage is one of the most important contributors to hedge fund returns. We would also expect that the greatest periods of hedge fund malaise will coincide with rapid or sudden changes in U.S. interest rates. In Chart 11.1 we contrast the changes in returns of an unweighted index of the returns of all the major hedge fund style indices and contrast these to changes in 3-month U.S.$ Libor rates, advanced by 3 months. In other words, we are looking to see how changes in interest rates will influence changes in hedge fund performance, 3 months later.

As we can see, from January 1994 to October 1998, there seems to be an extreme sensitivity of hedge fund performance. Changes in 3-month U.S.$ Libor interest rates seem to be quite closely connected to changes in hedge fund performance 3 months later. Furthermore, the faster and larger the change (positive or negative) to interest rates, the greater the change in overall hedge fund performance. Clearly this connection must occur through the workings of leverage that we described earlier. Increases in interest rates reduce the value of the securities placed as collateral with the banks. Falling collateral generates margin calls, forcing funds to either close or liquidate their positions.

In light of the apparent sensitivity of hedge funds to changes in interest rates, through the amount of leverage they use, investors should use extra care in adding hedge funds to a portfolio containing other interest-rate-sensitive assets. This is not a minor issue if we consider that in today's financial markets, three of the other components of traditional institutional portfolios—stocks, bonds, and real estate—have strong but varying sensitivity to interest rates.

A true bear market caused by a reversal in the present trend of declining nominal interest rates could have serious implications for the attractiveness of hedge funds as a diversification tool in an investor's portfolio, a point alluded to in Chap. 2 text and illustrated in Charts 2.1 and 2.2.

CHART 11.1

Changes in hedge fund returns versus 3-month U.S. Libor rates January 1994 to October 1998.

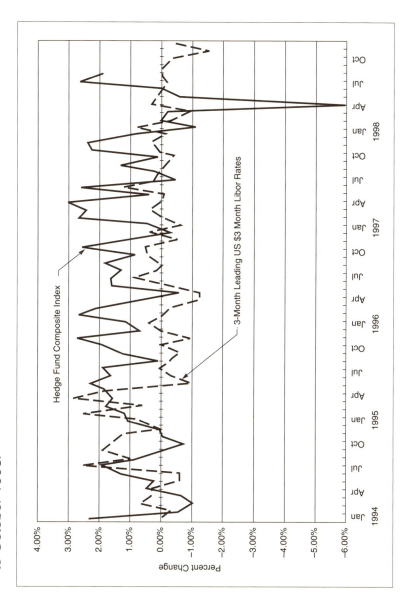

Source: Lara Capital and Hfr.

CHAPTER 12

Case Study of a Real-World Hedge Fund

So far much of what we have covered has tended to be of an abstract or theoretical nature, which would be interesting to apply to a real-life hedge fund. We have, therefore, selected as a case the performance of the Global Systems Fund managed by Victor Niederhoffer. Our analysis will cover the period from January 1993 to October 1997 when, owing to a series of bad positions, the fund lost all of its investor's assets. Admittedly, we will be working with 20/20 hindsight. All the same, given the wide variety of outcomes in the performance of Global Systems' track record we'll be able to review and cover a wide array of situations. The fund's track record is produced in Table 12.1 and its cumulative returns are illustrated in Chart 12.1.

Global Systems was a hedge fund dedicated to trading international markets based on a blend of technical indicators and Victor Niederhoffer's own sense of the markets. Its style, in other words, was that of a high-risk, high-return investment vehicle, which at times used substantial leverage to achieve its investment aims. This is confirmed by Chart 12.2 which illustrates both the changes in the Global Systems net asset value and its rolling quarterly standard deviation (expressed as percent per annum).

In looking at the upper half of Chart 12.2, we notice the wide swings in the d ratio, confirmed by the oscillations of

TABLE 12.1

Track Record (Net Asset Value) of Global Systems Fund, January 1993 to October 1997

Month	Value	Month	Value	Month	Value	Month	Value	Month	Value
Jan-93	2.540%	Jan-94	2.030%	Jan-95	6.270%	Jan-96	6.250%	Jan-97	4.740%
Feb-93	0.680%	Feb-94	3.130%	Feb-95	3.090%	Feb-96	7.030%	Feb-97	−2.620%
Mar-93	−2.520%	Mar-94	7.620%	Mar-95	−0.900%	Mar-96	5.640%	Mar-97	−2.130%
Apr-93	−1.560%	Apr-94	5.010%	Apr-95	2.620%	Apr-96	5.640%	Apr-97	2.430%
May-93	3.560%	May-94	9.650%	May-95	3.350%	May-96	3.030%	May-97	−5.180%
Jun-93	−3.710%	Jun-94	7.890%	Jun-95	2.330%	Jun-96	1.480%	Jun-97	−8.360%
Jul-93	0.250%	Jul-94	1.660%	Jul-95	−11.170%	Jul-96	1.830%	Jul-97	4.930%
Aug-93	−4.540%	Aug-94	1.120%	Aug-95	0.180%	Aug-96	3.000%	Aug-97	−46.100%
Sep-93	7.580%	Sep-94	2.960%	Sep-95	2.950%	Sep-96	5.560%	Sep-97	26.260%
Oct-93	−0.020%	Oct-94	2.930%	Oct-95	2.700%	Oct-96	2.970%	Oct-97	−100.000%
Nov-93	5.960%	Nov-94	5.850%	Nov-95	4.500%	Nov-96	−0.370%		
Dec-93	1.020%	Dec-94	1.720%	Dec-95	2.120%	Dec-96	−2.890%		

Source: Lara Capital and Bank Julius Bär.

CHART 12.1

Global Systems cumulative monthly returns, January 1993 to October 1997

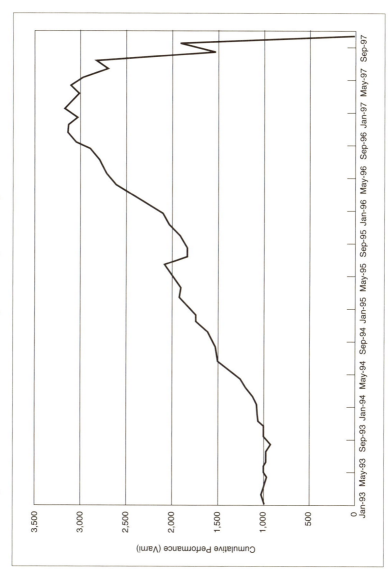

Source: Lara Capital and Bank Julius Bär.

139

CHART 12.2

Global Systems monthly returns and quarterly standard deviations, January 1993 to October 1997

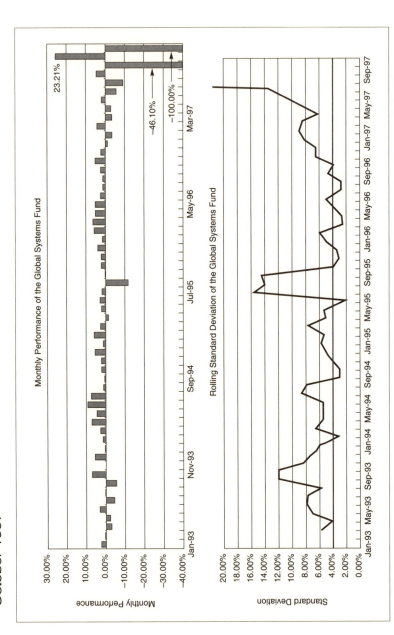

Source: Lara Capital and Bank Julius Bär.

the fund's annualized quarterly standard deviation numbers in the lower half. There can be little doubt this is a very volatile vehicle.

We'll continue our analysis by looking at the fund's performance during 1993, the first year of our track record. Our objective is to see what we can derive from this year's worth of data. We also want to see if it is consistent with both the fund's prospectus, and with the performance of other managers in the same investment style (peer group). To make our analysis and comparisons meaningful, we will risk-adjust our data first by subtracting the total returns of the 3-month U.S. T-bill from our track record numbers, and then subtract the performance of an index of macro hedge fund manager performance.

To get an idea of the risk/reward tradeoff underlying the fund's performance, let us look at Chart 12.3, where we illustrate the distribution of returns we get after adjusting our returns for the risk-free rate. In 1993 the returns were skewed, consistent with our expectation of hedge fund returns. However, contrary to expectations, the skew is both minor and toward the negative, rather than the positive. Over 66 percent of Global Systems' returns were between zero and -0.5 percent, and only 33 percent of its returns were greater than zero. This would seem to imply that in 1993 Global Systems provided us with little value-added when compared to a risk-free T-bill. Although the negative skew could mean that statistics relying on the assumption of normality would have underestimated the true risk of investing in Global Systems, this error is quite small, as shown by the superimposed normal distribution in Chart 12.3.

This means that we could safely approximate the distribution of a manager's returns with a normal distribution. However, as we saw in Chaps. 8 and 10, this would point to the possibility of the fund providing little value-added to the investor since randomness, rather than skill, could be a great source of the fund's returns. This would also mean that there is potential for the fund to generate large and unexpected losses for the investor.

CHART 12.3

Global Systems distribution of risk-adjusted returns, 1993.

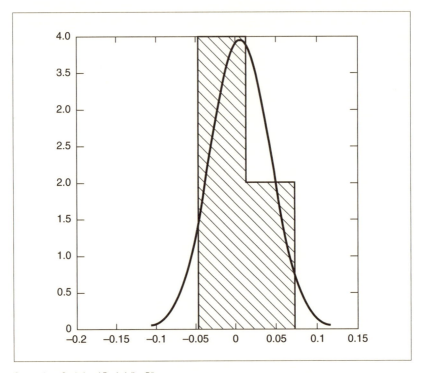

Source: Lara Capital and Bank Julius Bär.

We can conclude that during 1993 Global Systems was not providing investors with adequate value-added for the risks inherent in the vehicle. We now need to try to find out what could have been the cause of this performance: poor skill, poor risk management, or a difficult market. This will allow us to increase the effectiveness of our questions to the manager during the course of a due-diligence interview.

To develop some clues as to whether the 1993 performance was attributable to the manager or the market environment, we can look at how Global Systems performed in comparison to its manager's peers. To do this, let's look at the distribution of the risk- and peer-group-adjusted returns, shown in Chart 12.4.

From the chart we can see that during 1993 Global Systems' returns provided little true value-added with respect to its peers. About 57 percent of the manager's returns were identical to those of the peer group. Of the balance, around 20 percent were better and about 23 percent were worse than those of the peer group. The manager thus appears to have performed slightly worse than those in the peer group. The wider dispersion of the manager's returns relative to those of the peer group also points to higher leverage than the peer group. However, this leverage is not being used effectively. A d ratio of 1.15 and the slight negative skew confirm this, as seen in Chart 12.4.

This analysis would appear to contradict our earlier hypothesis, that Global Systems is being run by a good manager

CHART 12.4

Global Systems distribution of risk- and peer-group-adjusted returns, 1993.

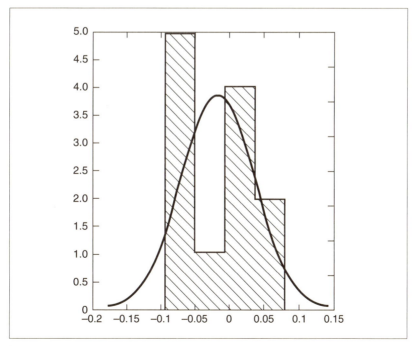

Source: Lara Capital and Bank Julius Bär.

facing an adverse market. Our data seem to suggest that we are faced with a manager who uses higher leverage, but less effectively than the peer group. The more pronounced skew in the returns for the fund also indicated that we could have problems in comparing it to other funds in the same peer group using statistics such as standard deviation or the Sharpe ratio.

Finally, Global System's returns appear to be heavily dependent on random factors over skills to generate their returns. This is confirmed by a Hurst index of almost 0.50 for 1993. This coefficient confirms that we are in the presence of a manager whose activities may expose investors to randomness in order to generate returns. This means that investors could face substantial losses should the 1993 performance be extended into future years.

Putting all the facts together, we must conclude that Global Systems is a highly speculative vehicle which uses higher leverage to provide lower risk-adjusted returns than its peers. Furthermore, the apparent dependence on random factors to generate its returns would appear to suggest that the fund might face greater-than-average risk of loss. This would lead us to conclude that it is not a good investment, compared to other funds in its peer group, since such a manager would offer little value-added to an investor.

Let us now assume that, despite the red flags thrown up by our analysis of the 1993 data, we had gone ahead and invested in Global Systems. During the following years, in line with our predictions derived from the 1993 data, Global Systems' returns fluctuated wildly.

The manager's ongoing reliance on randomness is evidenced by the wild swings in the fund's quarterly annualized d ratios reproduced in Chart 12.5. The fund's Hurst index, shown in Chart 12.6, while less volatile, swings between 0.5 and 0.4, indicating an ongoing influence of randomness in the generation of a manager's returns.

Looking at Chart 12.6, we also notice a substantial change in the behavior of the fund's Hurst index after July 1995. After

CHART 12.5

Global Systems rolling quarterly variations d ratio, January 1993 to October 1997.

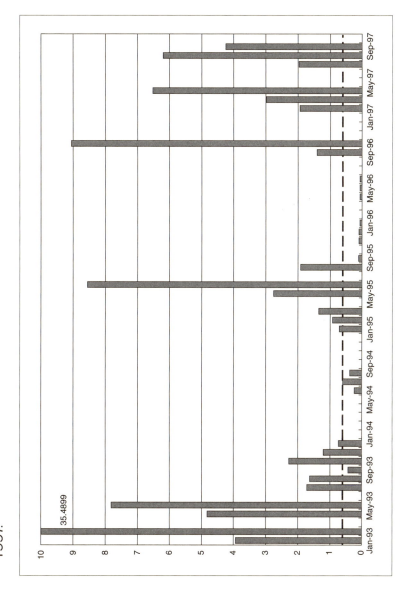

Source: Lara Capital and Bank Julius Bär.

CHART 12.6

Global Systems rolling quarterly variations Hurst index, January 1993 to October 1997.

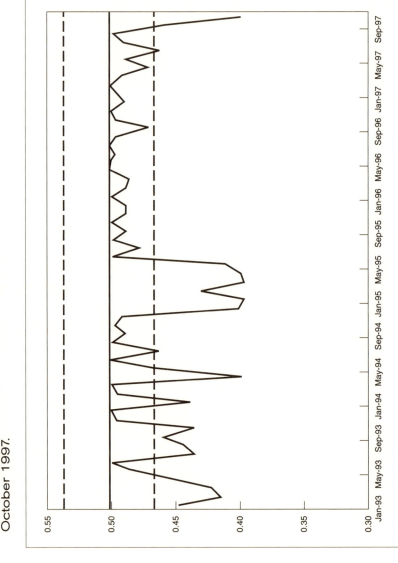

Source: Lara Capital and Bank Julius Bär.

that date it starts to fluctuate in an even narrower band around 0.5. We also note from Chart 12.5 that our d ratio gapped (i.e., assumed an infinite value) around the same date. This means that the manager must have incurred a substantial loss, which may have caused a change in the manager's subsequent activities. A review of Table 12.1 reveals that Global Systems lost over 11 percent in the month of July 1995, confirming our assumption of a landmark event on that date.

To understand how this event may have influenced the fund's performance, let us contrast changes in the fund's d ratio with its monthly performance, shown in Chart 12.7. This gives us an idea as to the relationship between monthly returns and changes in the behavior of the manager's Hurst index.

It is clear from Chart 12.7 that the manager's performance has changed in a substantial manner following July 1995. We do not know what precisely happened on that date, since we were not able to discuss the cause of this loss and the manager's subsequent activities with this manager personally. However, a clue emerges from Niederhoffer's book *The Education of a Speculator,* (Wiley, New York, 1997) which opens by talking about being "over his head" in a wrong way on a U.S. $300 million, dollar-yen currency-related bet. Interestingly, the book mentions that the profitability of the position depended on certain values of the dollar-yen. Oddly enough, those values of the exchange rate were unique and match those prevailing around June–July 1995.

Whatever the cause for the loss, Charts 12.4 and 12.5 seem to indicate that following this event there was either a radical change in the manager's investment style, or in the underlying markets, to which the manager did not adjust. Following the July 1995 loss, the manager's monthly returns worsen and this manager's returns become almost entirely dependent on random events, and thus more volatile.

This shift is confirmed by Chart 12.8, which shows the distribution of the manager's risk- and peer-group-adjusted returns during 1996. In particular, looking at the chart, we note

CHART 12.7

Global Systems monthly returns and Hurst index, January 1993 to October 1997.

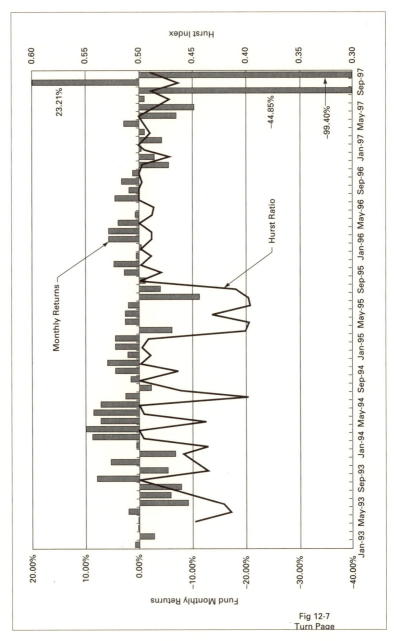

Fig 12-7
Turn Page

Source: Lara Capital and Bank Julius Bär.

C H A R T   12.8

Global Systems distribution of risk- and peer-group-adjusted returns, 1993.

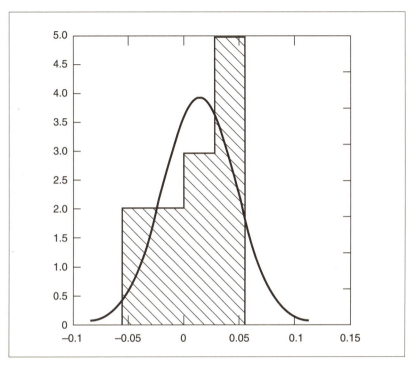

Source: Lara Capital and Bank Julius Bär.

that now 25 percent of the manager's returns are similar to those of the peer group, 8 percent are lower, and almost 47 percent are higher. Although these returns definitely have a positive skew, they entail a large negative tail, as is confirmed by the superimposed normal distribution. This skew appears to be caused by leverage rather than skill, as indicated by both the skew and its wider dispersion and tails in the manager's returns, compared to those in the peer group.

Taken together, the disproportionate element of randomness in the manager's activities, the increased possibility for extreme events (outliers) in the manager's performance, and that manager's high leverage, increase the chances of investors facing serious risk of loss. One could almost say that the picture that emerges from these data is that of a manager trying to make up for losses and in so doing overreaching, probably violating many of the long-held and time-tested investment beliefs and strategies in the process. The ultimate result was that the manager lost all the investor's money.

Our data and tools seem to point to a complete breakdown in both the manager's value-added skill and risk management ability after 1995. Thus the wild fluctuations in the manager's d ratio and the narrow fluctuation in that manager's Hurst index around 0.5 were definite, screaming red flags. If the manager had exited in July 1995, an investor would have incurred losses, but would have avoided the entire loss of the manager's capital, as events later showed.

As we said, this case is being presented with 20/20 hindsight. It is, however, interesting to note the richness of the analysis that comes if one looks beyond the results derived from an analysis based on average returns and the dispersion of these returns around the mean.

CHAPTER 13

Conclusion: Putting It All Together

There are many who proclaim hedge funds as either "the next great thing" or the "great Satan" of financial markets. We hope the presentations in this book will allow our readers to cast a jaundiced eye on such exaggerated claims. First, we showed there is no such thing as an archetypal hedge fund on which to hang such sweeping generalizations. Second, such sweeping generalizations rarely answer the question of why hedge funds exist in the first place. Nor do they allow investors to understand why sophisticated investors of all stripes, from wealthy individuals to university endowments, entrust their money to these vehicles.

As investment vehicles that showcase and emphasize the skills of an investment manager, hedge funds can provide tremendous benefits to investors. Identifying these benefits, however, requires that investors develop an understanding of what to focus on. In this book we highlighted those aspects we felt are important, which can be summarized as follows:

- *Value-added.* Hedge funds are attractive investment vehicles provided they generate attractive, risk-adjusted returns for their investors, compared to other assets. This value-added can be either on a stand-alone basis or on a portfolio basis (i.e., its influence on the overall risk-adjusted returns of the investor's portfolio).

- *Manager skills.*   To generate value-added, hedge funds are heavily reliant on the manager's skills to exploit the tremendous flexibility typically offered by the fund's investment guidelines. The ability to go long or short, use leverage, and use derivative and select markets and entry points has a tremendous impact on the fund's performance. At the same time, this flexibility makes it harder for the investors to understand how a fund's returns are generated. There is no underlying reference asset to monitor or against which to benchmark the manager. Investors need to pay attention in isolating the effect of luck from skill in evaluating a manager's performance, since luck is inevitably a guarantee of investment losses. The key to this lies in identifying managers with stable skills.

- *Stability of skills.*   Hedge funds are dynamic vehicles operating in dynamic markets. To reap the full benefits of a manager's value-added, investors need to identify those managers who can deliver value-added in a consistent manner. Investors then need to monitor a manager's ongoing performance to ensure that there is no erosion of these skills over time. This requires using tools that highlight the dynamic component of hedge fund behavior.

- *Safety.*   The dynamics of hedge fund behavior, especially in the context of poor or slipping manager skills, can have serious implications on the safety of an investment in a hedge fund. Poor or slipping skills are closely linked to hedge fund losses, because of the laws of probability. Funds whose managers have low or falling skills appear to have extremely high mortality rates.

- *Interest rate sensitivity.*   Leverage is an integral component of hedge fund operations. Because of the way leverage is structured in a hedge fund, these vehicles have a greater sensitivity to interest rates than is commonly recognized. Furthermore, this sensitivity is not symmetrical. Hedge funds are much more susceptible to generating poor returns because of rising interest rates than they are in generating better performance because of falling ones.

In seeking to shed light on such issues, investors are limited by the flaws in many of the traditional tools used in hedge fund evaluation and monitoring. We can summarize these as follows:

- *Skews.*   Skilled fund managers tend to have distributions of returns that are skewed. Such skews bias the meaningfulness of average returns and standard deviations in measuring a fund's returns and risk.
- *Dynamics.*   Hedge funds are dynamic vehicles, designed to exploit the constant changes in the markets in which they operate. Static measurements, which translate a manager's performance into one number, do not effectively capture their true behavior.
- *Portfolio allocation.*   Hedge fund manager skills and the dynamics of hedge fund operations can distort the meaningfulness of correlation numbers in measuring hedge fund sensitivity to other assets. This also influences the effectiveness of using traditional portfolio diversification with hedge funds.

In this book we presented some tools and techniques investors can use to address these flaws. In particular, we outlined how rolling-window techniques allow investors to capture some of the feel and dynamics of hedge fund behavior. We saw that *d* ratios allow investors to exploit the skew in manager returns to identify better investment opportunities. The Hurst index allows investors to identify the stability in a manager's skill and the permanence of these skills over time. Finally, rethinking the traditional approach to portfolio allocation allows investors to create more effective portfolios. Despite these useful tools, investors should never forget that hedge fund investing remains more of an art than a science.

Sophisticated tools are often a poor substitute for common sense and a good understanding of the mechanics and realities of investing in today's markets. It is for this reason that we spent some time analyzing, in detail, the mechanical aspects of leverage in a hedge fund's operations. Hopefully this will give investors an understanding of how leverage can assist hedge fund performance, as well as the risks and special problems it entails for both the manager and the investor.

At present, one of the key obstacles in performing detailed hedge fund analysis is the lack of readily available information. However, the industry is growing rapidly. In 1990 there were about 70 hedge funds; today there are about 50,000. Under this onslaught the hedge fund industry is beginning to lose its insular, clubby characteristics. As competition for investor dollar increases, we believe that hedge fund transparency must inevitably increase. To get an idea of what the future will bring to transparency in the industry, one only has to witness the growth in the late 1990s of hedge fund information and hedge fund performance indices freely available from different servers on the Internet. Against the backdrop of increasing investments, it is inevitable that hedge funds, regardless of their investment styles, will segment in the search for returns. Some will grow and seek to utilize their size to capitalize on investment opportunities. Others will seek niches and choose to stay small and specialized. Regardless of the growth strategy chosen, competition for investor dollars and increased regulatory pressure will ensure that more information will become available to a wider audience in the near future. It is inevitable that we will see in the hedge fund industry a replay of the evolution seen in most other financial markets during the late 1980s and throughout the 1990s, when information became more available and more widely disseminated. Increased transparency led to greater investor inflow, which depressed returns. In turn, declining returns forced investors to adopt better analysis to identify newer profitable opportunities. This, in turn, forced greater transparency, and so on.

In the case of hedge funds, as investment dollars continue to flow into the industry, it is inevitable that risk-adjusted returns will continue to decline across all hedge fund investment styles. These declines will favor investors, who are able to make more effective decisions and evaluations. The declining returns will bring attention to the risks of hedge fund investing and the need to measure and quantify it accurately. Smart investors who understand this trend will be able to make, understand, and correctly evaluate both the risks of a hedge fund style and of a manager belonging to that group. This will allow an investor to identify and select the managers who provide the most effective combination of risk and return. In so doing they will avoid the inevitable bust cycles that will follow the present boom.

Despite the merits of hedge funds as skill-based investment vehicles, too many investors currently flock, sheeplike, into poorly understood hedge fund vehicles or investment styles. Their motives for investing are often no more sophisticated than the promises of untold riches, and their analyses simply a list of others who may hold the same investment. Certainly, market forces will fleece many of these investors. Funds that are subject to such large, unsophisticated investor inflows must inevitably face the return risk and the increased chance of generating losses for their investors.

Modestly, I hope that this book will go a long way toward placing my readers in the category of the savvy hedge fund managers rather than in that of the sheep.

Hedge Funds

HEDGE FUND STRUCTURE

Hedge funds are essentially collective investment vehicles. They are legal entities that allow different investors to pool their money, to be managed by an investment manager according to the terms and conditions outlined in the fund's offering document or prospectus.

These funds are established either as companies or partnerships. The partnerships, generally limited partnerships, under which investors' liabilities are limited to their investment in the company, are typically domiciled in the United States. The investment companies, in which the investor is just a regular shareholder (with limited or no voting power), are typically domiciled in jurisdictions with favorable taxation and financial regulation.

It is quite common for U.S.-based investment managers to have both a limited partnership, targeted toward domestic investors; and an offshore structure, targeted toward investors who are not resident in the United States. In exchange for lower or no regulation, such vehicles tend to be restricted to sophisticated and/or wealthy investors (for regulatory purposes, often the same thing), and for this reason tend to have high minimum investment levels. In evaluating any hedge fund, the key document an investor should obtain and read very carefully is the fund's offering document or prospectus. Aside from providing information on the manager's historical performance (track record), it should also contain information on

- *The fund's structure.*   How and where the fund is structured and located. It will also detail the form in which the investor's allocation will be evidenced (shares, etc.).
- *Eligible investors and sales restrictions.*   A definition of an eligible investor to whom the fund may be sold, including minimum net worth and domicile. The prospectus should also contain information on where the fund, for legal reasons, may not be sold.
- *Minimum investment amounts.*   To limit access to smaller investors, most hedge funds require large minimum investment amounts, which can vary between U.S. $250,000 and $1,000,000.
- *Fees, costs, and manager's remuneration.*   All the items that will reduce the investor's return in the fund. Careful attention should be paid to the nature and structure of these items and how and when they are computed, assessed, and deducted.
- *Investment strategy.*   How the fund intends to generate returns for investors, including what it may or may not invest in, the instruments it will use, how much it may borrow, and the maximum amount of leverage it may apply to its investment positions.
- *Revaluation procedures.*   With what frequency the fund's investments will be valued, with what frequency the value of the investor's position in the fund will be calculated, who shall be responsible for these procedures, and what sources will be used for pricing information.

- *Dividend and distribution policy.*   The manner and frequency with which distributions of profits and capital may be made to investors.
- *Applicable laws.*   The law under which the fund's activities will be governed and the law under which the funds investments may be subject.
- *Lockup periods.*   Periods during which investors may not liquidate their investments in the fund.
- *Redemption frequency and procedures.*   Following a lockup period, if applicable, the frequency and manner in which such redemption may be made, whom to instruct, and the amount of time it will take for an investor to secure the return on an investment.
- *General risk factors associated with the fund's operations.* Although generally boilerplate, it should contain information on such issues as counterparty risk and market illiquidity, which may have a considerable impact on the investor, should they ever come into play.
- *Other commercial relationships.*   Commercial or fee-sharing relationships the fund has with other entities which may or may not be related to the fund, the investment manager, or other agents in the fund's activities. All too often this information is provided in very cursory form, and if not detailed in the prospectus, investors should always seek explicit information on this point.

The prospectus will also contain information on the following agents (others are listed in Chart A1.1) who are involved in the fund's operations. The agents indicated as optional do not appear in all hedge funds, as their role or other agents may subsume function.

- *Sponsor or promoter (optional).*   The individual or group who is responsible for marketing and providing client services for the fund.

CHART A 1.1

Relationship between the different entities involved in the operation of in a "typical" hedge fund.

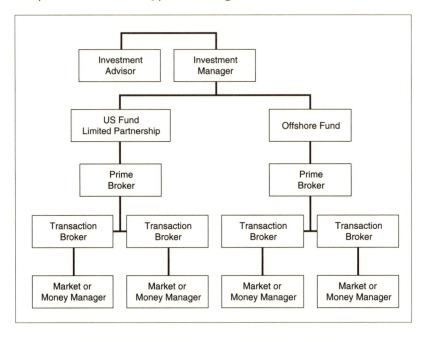

- *Investment advisor* (*optional*).   The individual or group who assists the investment manager with the implementation of the investment strategy. In many funds the roles of investment manager and investment advisor are covered by the same individual or company.

- *Fund manager* (*optional*).   The individual or group responsible for investing funds on behalf of the investment manager. This agent is prevalent in funds of funds where the investment manager's mandate is to invest in other funds. Other funds may allocate investments to outside managers. Care should be taken in reading the prospectus to understand the exact nature of the relationship between the fund and the outside manager.

- *Investment manager.* The individual or group who designs the investment strategy and oversees its implementation. If no detailed information is given in the prospectus, the investment manager may also perform the roles of sponsor, fund manager, and investment advisor. When in doubt, the investor should always seek clarification.

- *Fund administrator.* The individual or group that is responsible for processing investor's subscriptions and redemptions. The fund administrator is also responsible for calculating the value of the investor's holdings, either as an NAV or as a partnership share.

- *Custodian.* The financial entity responsible for holding the assets of the fund, which controls and monitors the flow of capital to meet margin needs.

- *Prime broker.* The main financial entity through which the fund manager and/or the investment advisor coordinates the allocation of funds to different brokers and settles the different transactions on their behalf. The prime broker is also the key entity through which the fund's borrowing and collateral (supporting this borrowing) is managed.

- *Transaction broker.* The financial entity through which the fund manager and/or the investment advisor executes the investment activities.

To better understand how these different agents interact, let's run through three examples of a fund's operations.

Chart A1.2 shows what happens when an investor makes an initial investment in a fund. The investor pays the subscription into the custodian. The custodian confirms receipt of the funds to the administrator, who then proceeds to instruct the fund to issue shares to the investor. The fund administrator will now issue regular reports to the investor on the status of the investment. Once this investment is made, the fund is ready to invest.

CHART A1.2

What happens when an investor buys shares in a
"typical" hedge fund.

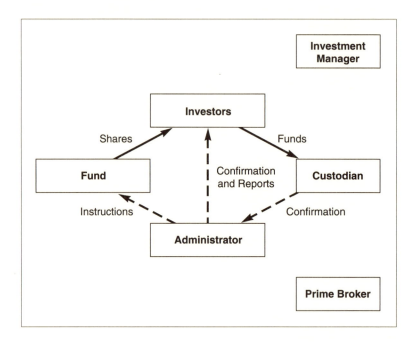

The fund is now ready to invest. The investment manager
gives instructions to move some assets from the custodian to
the prime broker, from where they will be invested in the market. Chart A1.3 outlines the flow of funds in this case. Both the
prime broker and the custodian will report their transactions to
the administrator, who will keep track of them for the regular
reporting to the investor.

At redemption as shown in Chart A1.4, the flow of Chart
A1.2 is reversed. Having liquidated the positions, the prime
broker transfers the liquidity to the custodian, under advice of
the administrator. The administrator then awaits confirmation
of the receipt of the shares to instruct the custodian to return
funds to the investor.

CHART A1.3

What happens when the investment manager acts in a
"typical" hedge fund.

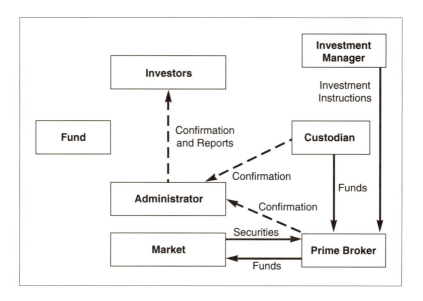

CHART A1.4

What happens when an investor sells shares in a
"typical" hedge fund.

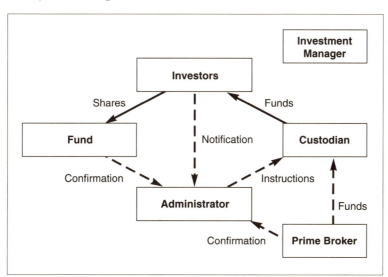

Distributions

NORMAL DISTRIBUTIONS

Most of the statistical tools used in evaluating hedge funds make use of the so-called normal or gaussian distribution. This distribution is the foundation of the statistical analysis of many random events or phenomenon, from signal processing to test scoring. Its enormous popularity is due to a series of factors: (1) many random events *do* follow, or can readily be approximated by, a normal distribution; (2) a normal distribution is easy to handle mathematically, with many useful properties that can simplify its practical application; and (3) it is difficult to ignore the force of convention and habit. Often the assumption of a process following a normal distribution has to do with the fact that it is the core of many basic canned statistical software applications. Its application is the result of laziness or habit, rather than conscious choice. One well-known physicist, exasperated about this situation, described it in the following terms: "The experimenters like to use it because they think the theorists have proved its universal applicability. The theorists use it because they think the experimenters have proved its applicability to the real world." Because of built-in inertia, normal distributions are frequently used in situations where they are not applicable, often with disastrous results.

One of the most attractive features of the normal distribution is that, given a data series of elements X_i and length n, once we know the mean and standard deviation of this data series we can derive the rest of the distribution through the following formula:

$$G = \frac{1}{\sigma \sqrt{2\Pi}} \cdot \exp\left[\frac{-(x - \mu)^2}{2\sigma^2} \right] \qquad \text{(A2.1)}$$

where μ is the distribution mean given by $\sum X_i / N$ and σ is the distribution variance given by $\sum (X_i - \mu)^2 / N$.

Normal distributions are generally associated with random processes that have equal likelihood of outcome. A classic example is the behavior of a market over a 60-day period as reproduced in Table A2.1, during which period the market was up for 33 days out of 60 on average (i.e., it was up 55.7 percent of the time). The average return for the period was 0.05 and the total return to an investor in this market would have been 3. Although such a market has a very slight skew as evidenced by a d coefficient of 7.4, a normal distribution with a mean of 0.05, and a standard deviation of 1.43 can approximate it, as shown in Chart A2.1.

In Table A2.1 we can see that the returns fluctuate between -2 and $+2$, so the distribution we can derive is symmetrical, as is the superimposed normal distribution in Chart A2.1.

NORMAL DISTRIBUTIONS AND SAMPLING

For the purposes of evaluating hedge funds, the single most powerful property of a normal distribution is the *central-limit theorem*, which, in simple terms, states that, should the underlying process follow a normal distribution, any sample extracted from that distribution will also follow a normal distribution. Furthermore, should samples be taken, any deviations we encounter between the distribution of this sample and the distribution of the overall population will be small enough over

T A B L E   A 2.1

Behavior of a Random Market Over a 60-Day Period

Day	Direction	Move	Day	Direction	Move	Day	Direction	Move
1	Down	−1	21	Down	−1	41	Up	0
2	Down	−2	22	Down	−1	42	Up	2
3	Down	−1	23	Down	−1	43	Up	2
4	Up	1	24	Up	1	44	Down	−1
5	Up	0	25	Down	−1	45	Up	1
6	Up	2	26	Up	1	46	Down	−1
7	Down	−2	27	Down	−1	47	Up	0
8	Up	1	28	Up	2	48	Down	−2
9	Up	2	29	Down	−1	49	Up	1
10	Up	0	30	Down	−1	50	Up	1
11	Down	−2	31	Down	−1	51	Down	−1
12	Up	1	32	Down	−2	52	Up	2
13	Down	−2	33	Up	2	53	Down	−1
14	Up	2	34	Down	−2	54	Up	2
15	Up	0	35	Up	1	55	Down	−2
16	Up	0	36	Up	2	56	Down	−1
17	Up	1	37	Up	0	57	Down	−2
18	Down	−1	38	Up	1	58	Up	2
19	Down	−1	39	Up	1	59	Down	−2
20	Up	2	40	Up	1	60	Up	2

time to be ignored. Applied to the context of hedge funds, this can tell us two things:

1. Should the fund rely on the underlying market for the bulk of its returns (e.g., in the case of a mutual fund or a low-skill hedge fund), then the distributions of these returns will follow a normal distribution, if the returns of that market are normally distributed.
2. Should we extract any sample of returns from a manager's track record that is normally distributed, than these sample returns will also be normally distributed.

CHART A2.1

The normal distribution derived from the data in
Table A2.1.

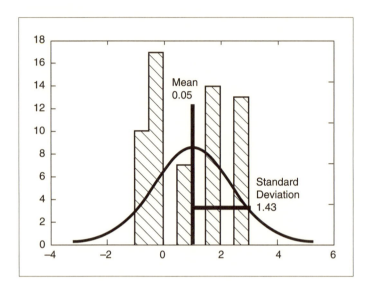

It is the central-limit theorem that allows quantitative analysis of manager track records to assume normal distributions of returns. However, as we noted, for this theorem to work its magic, the underlying distribution must follow that of a normal distribution. In the case of many hedge funds, this is simply not true, since hedge fund returns exhibit skews, tails, and in some cases multiple humps (also called *multimodal distributions*), all of which are incompatible with a normal distribution. In such cases the errors that the nonnormality can inflict on hedge fund results are unpredictable, and have to be seen on a case-by-case basis.

NORMAL DISTRIBUTIONS AND FAT TAILS

A normal distribution is a distribution that is extremely compact and is not compatible with "outliers," extreme events that are outside the range of the other data. Under a normal distribution, two-thirds of all outcomes associated with the distribution fall within ±1 SD from the mean, while 95 percent of the outcomes associated with the distribution fall within ±2 SD from the mean. We can use this property of a normal distribution to say that less than 5 percent of the outcome falls outside ±2 SD from the population mean. This means that in most cases these extreme events or outliers are small enough to be ignored.[1] Should this not be the case, the distribution is said to have "fat tails." Many financial markets seem to exhibit a greater frequency of extreme events than is predicted by a normal distribution. For this reason there has been a growing body of financial literature pointing to the fact that fat tails are an inherent characteristic in the financial markets.

NORMAL DISTRIBUTIONS, KURTOSIS, AND SKEWNESS

Skewness

Skewness characterizes the degree of asymmetry of a distribution around its mean. Traditionally distribution skewness has been measured by the following formula:

$$ S = \frac{N}{(N-1) \cdot (N-2)} \cdot \frac{\sum_{i}^{n} (X_i - \mu)^3}{\sigma^3} \qquad \text{(A2.2)} $$

where μ = distribution mean given by $\sum X_i / N$
σ = distribution variance given by $\sum (X_i - \mu)^2 / N$
N = length of our data series
X_i = ith element in our data series

---

[1] Because few financial asset prices go below zero, often a log of the normal distribution is used when modeling financial markets. This is the so-called log-normal distribution. The two distributions are closely related, as one is merely the log of the other. For this reason, the log-normal distribution preserves many of the attractive mathematical properties of a normal distribution, and does not warrant a separate discussion here.

Positive skewness indicates a distribution with an asymmetrical tail extending toward more positive values. *Negative skewness* indicates a distribution with an asymmetrical tail extending toward more negative values. Although the sign of the skewness coefficient will tell us about the direction of the skew, the coefficient, per se, provides us with little unique information about the skew. Many different distributions can have the same skew coefficient. For this reason we preferred to focus on the *d* ratio in evaluating hedge funds. The *d* ratio is easier to compute and gave us interesting information on a distribution's skew. As Chart A2.2 shows, the *d* coefficient and the skew coefficient derived from Table A2.1 are closely related.

Kurtosis

Kurtosis characterizes the relative peakedness or flatness of a distribution compared with the normal distribution. Traditionally, kurtosis is calculated by the following formula:

$$K = \left(\frac{N - (N + 1)}{[(N - 1) \cdot (N - 2) \cdot (N - 3)]} \right) \cdot \sum_{i}^{n} \frac{(X_i - \mu)^4}{\sigma^4} \quad \text{(A2.3)}$$

where μ = distribution mean given by $\sum_i X_i / N$
σ = distribution variance given by $\mu(X_i - \mu)^2 / N$
N = length of our data series
X_i = ith element in our data series

Positive kurtosis indicates a relatively peaked distribution. *Negative kurtosis* indicates a relatively flat distribution. The degree of kurtosis can give us some idea as to the shape and type of tails present in a distribution. In this book we have chosen to make no use of the coefficient of kurtosis in our analysis, as it is not a unique measurement of the "tailedness" of a distribution. Instead, we have preferred to rely on heuristic methods of detecting a skew using graphical analysis and the analysis of other coefficients like the Hurst coefficient, *d* ratio, and standard deviation.

CHART A2.2

Comparison between d ratio and coefficient of skewness.

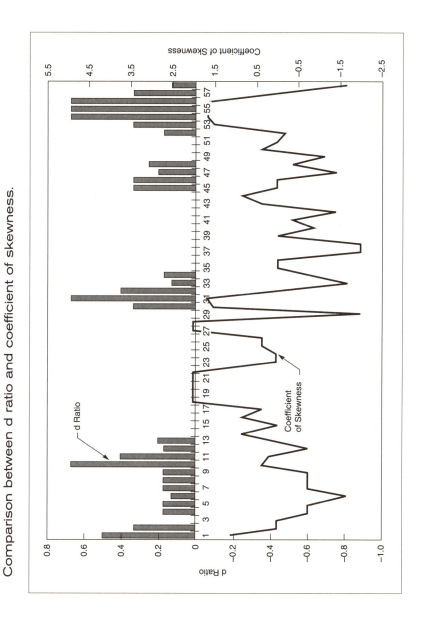

TABLE A2.2

A Comparison of the Kurtosis, Hurst, and Standard
Deviation Coefficients of the Major Hedge Fund Groups

	Kurtosis	Hurst	Standard Deviation
Macro	0.101662	0.331585	0.033489
Market timing	−0.09181	0.345564	0.035744
Equity hedge	0.414554	0.416839	0.046044
Convertible arbitrage	0.546952	0.419554	0.029257
Emerging market	1.189829	0.443483	0.031744
Market-neutral	0.459774	0.453115	0.038644
Merger	3.73841	0.475154	0.044948
Event-driven	2.199533	0.477709	0.038699
Distressed	2.894891	0.479532	0.04386
Relative value	3.628565	0.480771	0.036379
Mortgage	6.737006	0.494584	0.043049

Source: Lara Capital and Hfr.

Table A2.2 compares kurtosis with the Hurst and standard deviation coefficients for the major hedge fund types. Consistent with our expectations, funds with the highest Hurst coefficient (the greatest degree of randomness and conformity to a normal distribution) also have the highest kurtosis coefficient that indicates a "peaky" distribution. Those with the lowest Hurst coefficient seem to have the lowest kurtosis coefficient. However, as Table A2.2 shows, it is impossible to make any further generalizations.

NORMAL DISTRIBUTIONS AND THE RELIABILITY OF HEDGE FUND STATISTICS

Tails and skews in the distribution of a hedge fund's returns will also influence some basic tools used to measure a hedge fund's performance. This is because many of these statistics implicitly assume a normal distribution of returns. The statistics that can be most influenced by this are described in the following paragraphs.

The Standard Deviation as a Proxy for Risk

Should hedge fund data be skewed, tailed, or multimodal, it is highly probable that 95 percent of our data will not be within ±2 SD of our mean. Depending on the nature of the defect, the classic standard deviation will either over- or underestimate the dispersion of data around the mean, and thus the fund's risk. This also means that fund risk ranking based on standard deviation are misleading, since the statistic may be flawed.

The Sharpe Ratio as a Tool for Ranking Funds

There are many ways of calculating a Sharpe ratio. The most common method is to take a fund's risk-adjusted average returns and divide them by the standard deviation of these returns. The Sharpe ratio is thus simply a reward/risk ratio. However, in the case of hedge fund data that is skewed, tailed, or multimodal, a fund's mean and standard deviation of returns may be misrepresenting the fund's true characteristics in terms of returns and risk. This also means that fund risk rankings based on standard deviation are misleading, since the statistic may be flawed.

The Van Ratio as a Tool for Measuring Fund Riskiness

Developed by George Van of Van Hedge Fund Advisors, the Van ratio takes a different approach to measuring hedge fund risk. Using the compact property of a normal distribution, the Van ratio calculates the probability of loss associated with a hedge fund's return. It is calculated by taking the average yearly standard return for a manager and dividing it by the average of standard deviation over the year's four quarters. A

20 percent Van ratio for a manager in the past year tells us that there is a one-in-five chance that the manager may face a loss during the next year. The predictive power of this ratio derives from the compact properties of a normal distribution. However, should the data be skewed, tailed, or multimodal, then we can no longer be confident, either that the central-limit theorem will apply or that 95 percent of the data will be contained ±2 SD of the mean. In such cases the information supplied by the Van ratio will be meaningless.

Risk Diversification

THE POWER OF CORRELATION IN RISK DIVERSIFICATION

In Chap. 3 we saw that, as the basis for diversification, correlation appeared to be the less "costly" and thus the most promising risk management tool. Given its importance in finance and its implications to hedge fund investing, it warrants further attention, especially since it is at the core of most risk models and methodologies in use by many hedge funds and other sophisticated financial entities.

At the core of any diversification of financial assets are three key concepts: risk, return, and correlation. As an investor seeking to effectively diversify my portfolio, I will always select a combination of assets or positions that provides me with the most return for the least risk (the highest expected average return for the lowest standard deviation of these returns). I can achieve this objective through the magic of correlation, or the degree with which one asset rises or falls in regard to another.

Diversifying a portfolio based on correlation intuitively ensures that not all the assets in my portfolio change in value, by the same amount, at the same time. When some increase in value, others will decrease, smoothing out or stabilizing changes in my portfolio's overall value.

The *correlation coefficient* is the number that describes this relationship between two assets. It is defined as the percentage of movement in one asset that can be attributed to another. This coefficient will be expressed as a number that can assume values between -1 (perfect negative correlation) to $+1$ (perfect positive correlation), with the value zero indicating no significant correlation between the assets. Positively correlated assets will move in the same direction; negatively correlated assets will move in opposite directions.

Traditionally, the correlation coefficient Cxy between two assets with data series X and Y of length N has to be determined by the following formula:

$$Cxy = \frac{1}{N} \cdot \frac{\sum_{i}^{n} (X_i - \mu_x) \cdot (Y_i - \mu_y)}{\sigma_x \sigma_y} \qquad \text{(A3.1)}$$

where μ_x = distribution mean given by $\sum X_i / N$
μ_y = distribution mean given by $\sum Y_i / N$
σ_x = distribution variance given by $\sum (X_i - \mu)^2 / N$
σ_y = distribution variance given by $\sum (y_i - \mu)^2 / N$
N = length of our data series
X_i = ith element in our data series
Y_i = ith element in our data series

A well-diversified portfolio will contain assets with low or negative correlation to one another. However, there is no free lunch in using correlation to diversify a portfolio. In diversifying our portfolio through correlation, we are capping our upside (by ensuring that not all our assets rise by the same amount at the same time) in exchange for stability (by ensuring that not all our assets fall by the same amount at the same time).

For correlation-based diversification to work, the assets in our portfolio must

1. Be consistently and continuously negatively or poorly correlated over time
2. Have average return statistics that are meaningful
3. Have standard deviation statistics that are meaningful
4. Have correlation statistics that are meaningful

Many hedge funds violate these assumptions by virtue of their dynamic behavior (nonmeaningful correlation numbers) and the nonnormality in the distribution of their returns (nonmeaningful average returns and standard deviations). This means that my portfolio could be incorrectly diversified—either concentrated in closely correlated assets (thus having more risk than optimal) or overdiversified into poorly correlated assets (thus having less return than optimal).

The Hurst Index

A HISTORY OF THE HURST INDEX

In Egypt, since the times of the ancient Pharaohs, the size and timing of the annual flooding of the river Nile has perplexed the peoples who lived on its banks and depended on its bounty to survive. In the 1920s a British hydrologist, H. E. Hurst (1900–1978), was given the thankless task of trying to calculate the optimal storage capacity of water reservoirs on the river Nile. Because of the Nile's erratic cycles of flooding, solving this problem required trying to detect a possible pattern in the size and frequency of these floods. In trying to solve this problem, Hurst stumbled across a tool that has since been named after him, the *Hurst index*. One of the most important aspects of the Hurst index is the amount of information it can give a user on the variability and repeatability of a time series, without the need to make any assumptions about the nature of the underlying distribution. It is for this reason that, over the years, the Hurst exponent has progressed from a hydrological curiosity to become an important tool in the analysis of nonlinearity and randomness in many fields.

In the context of hedge fund evaluation, the Hurst index can be considered as obtaining information about a track record's tendency to fluctuate around a certain average value, without making any assumptions about the behavior of the underlying variables. Using the Hurst index allows us to circumvent many of the shortcoming ties to normal distribution when performing numerical analysis of hedge funds.

DERIVING THE HURST INDEX FROM HEDGE FUND TRACK RECORDS

To ensure that the data are consistent and comparable across managers, it is best to renormalize our excess manager's return data using what is called the *R/S algorithm*. To do this, we simply subdivide our manager's track record into a series of smaller time periods of length N, which suit our particular needs. For each of these t shorter periods we then compute the range for this time period $R(t)$, which is given by the difference between the highest and lowest values over the period as shown in the following formula:

$$R(t) = \max(t) - \min(t) \qquad (A4.1)$$

where $\max(t)$ is the maximum value of the data over the period t we have selected and $\min(t)$ is the minimum value of the data over the period t we have selected.

We then take the range $R(t)$ that we have computed and divide it by the standard deviation of the data over the selected subperiod t, $S(t)$. Our renormalized data will thus be given by

$$M(t) = \frac{R(t)}{S(t)} \qquad (A4.2)$$

Having renormalized our data through Eq. (A4.2), we can compute our Hurst index by solving the following formula for H:

$$\log(M) = \log(a) + H \cdot \log(N) \qquad (A4.3)$$

where $\log(M) = \log\left[R(t)/S(t)\right]$
      $\log(a)$ $= $ constant

$\log(N)$ = log of length or number of observations in data series t

Solving for H, this yields

$$H = \frac{\log(M)}{\log(n) - \log(a)} \qquad \text{(A4.4)}$$

In the case of hedge funds, with track records of 5 years or less, the value of $\log(a)$ can be assumed as sufficiently negligible to be ignored, giving us a handy way of determining the Hurst index for a hedge fund.

Risk-Free Rates and Peer-Group Index

In analyzing hedge funds, we have made use of two benchmarks or indices which warrant some greater attention: the risk-free rate and the peer-group index.

RISK-FREE RATES

The *risk-free rate* is the rate of interest I should expect to receive on a riskless investment. As such, it represents simply the pure "time value of money."

In countries where the rule of law is observed, where governments tend not to expropriate the public's savings or renege on their debt to the public, one can be relatively certain of being repaid by the government at maturity. This makes the country's short-term government debt "safe." Furthermore, if this country has a liquid government debt market, on which there are no legally imposed distortions on its workings, the interest rate on short-term government debt should represent the true "time value of money." This is the highest rate possible required covering an investor for the uncertainties of the future. Economists call such a rate the *risk-free rate,* because this is the rate of return the financial market expects for the uncertainty of the future, all other risks being absent. Any other investment should generally carry a premium to the risk-free rate, as it contains additional elements of risk aside from time. Stated in another way, any investment yielding more than the T-bill rate should contain additional elements of risk, or at least the perception of additional risk, on the part of the investing public.

Given its role as a proxy for the true time value of money, the returns on government short-term debt [U.S. Treasury bills (T-bills for short)] should be the meter against which financial performance should be measured. Let us suppose, for the sake of argument, that over the past 5 years U.S. 3-month T-bills have yielded a total return of 5 percent per annum. Clearly, if a manager over the past 5 years had generated an average return of 4.5 percent, after fees, it would be the same as saying that, unless other information is available, the manager provided investors with no value-added. Investors would have made more money by taking their investments and placing them in T-bills. Conversely, a manager making 20.00 percent on average over the past 5 years, assuming that the average total return on T-bills has been 5.00 percent, must have been undertaking a risk at least 4 times greater than the risk-free rate.

PEER-GROUP INDEX

This *peer-group index* is used to represent the returns we would have received had we invested in other managers who used the same investment style and/or operated in the same asset class as our manager. Using a peer-group index is a way of measuring the manager's performance with respect to other comparable funds.

Although this approach can yield many useful insights, it must be used with caution. Selecting and applying benchmark indices to a manager's performance is, unfortunately, not always straightforward. On one hand, there is the problem of finding a benchmark that "fits" the manager we are reviewing.

On the other hand, there is the problem of finding one that accurately reflects the peer group.

Realistically, no index will ever perform these functions in a satisfactory manner. Using an index will always require us to make some compromises. This makes the selection and application of indices more of an art than a science. Ultimately such factors as personal preference and gut feeling may well determine the use of one index over another. Because of this we must accept the fact that the results that we can derive from a peer-group-based analysis can never be precise, and that the information we derive from this process should be taken as an approximation rather than as hard facts.

The good news in using peer-group indices is that since the late 1990s there has been a proliferation of free hedge fund indices available for use from the Internet. This makes gaining access to peer-group index information relatively easy. It also gives us the luxury of being able to try different ready-made indices to find one that works the best. In this approach we should keep in mind a few important guidelines, which will ensure that our analysis will be meaningful and free from unnecessary biases:

1. Never use the benchmarks recommended by fund managers or their marketers.
2. Always know how the index was derived.
3. Never use an index if the manager is a member of the index, without removing that manager's impact on the index.
4. Always use an index composed of reputable managers with at least U.S. $100 million under management and at least a 5-year life.
5. Always ensure that the funds in the index are equally weighted.
6. Always ensure that the index is free from survivor bias.

Determining the appropriateness of an index for a hedge fund is an art. Nonetheless, the basic idea in the process will be to find a close fit between the distributions of manager returns and those of a peer group. As a starting point, one should try those that best represent one's investment style. If there is too large a discrepancy between this index and the manager's returns, only one of the following explanations can apply:

- The manager is misreporting the fund's activities (i.e., the manager's investments track another style).
- The manager is exceptionally talented.
- The manager's track record is fraudulent.

The first can easily be corrected by testing the manager's performance against other peer-group indices until one with a better fit is found. The other two cases can be found only through a careful review of the manager's activities in the due-diligence process.

Similarly, unexplainable differences between the manager's performance under different indices compiled for the same style group should be addressed with the manager, as these discrepancies may indicate style drift or other irregularities in the manager's behavior.

BIBLIOGRAPHY

Bennett, Deborah, *Randomness,* Harvard University Press, 1998.

Bernstein, Peter, *Against the Gods,* J. Wiley & Sons, New York, 1996.

Grimmett, G. R., and D. R. Stirzakor, *Profitability and Random Processes,* Oxford University Press, 1992.

Hedge Fund Research (HFR), www.HFR.com

Niherhoffer, Victor, *Educator of a Speculator,* J. Wiley & Sons, New York, 1997.

Peters, Edgar, *Chaos and Order in the Capital Markets,* J. Wiley & Sons, New York, 1991.

—, *Fractal Analysis,* J. Wiley & Sons, New York, 1994.

Schroder, Manfred, *Fractals Chaos and Power Laws,* W.H. Freeman & Co., 1991.

Van, George P., *Quantitative Analysis of Hedge Fund Return/Risk Characteristics,* Research paper, 1995, www.VanHedge.com

Van Hedge Fund Advisors, www.VanHedge.com

INDEX

Alternative investments/investment vehicles
 (*see* Hedge funds)
Analyzing hedge funds, 19–31
 historical returns in, 23–30
 prospectus in, 19–21, 25
 qualitative, 22–23
 quantitative, 22–23
Arbitrage, 2–3, 36
Arc-sine law, 120–121
Ax paradox, 28

Basis risk, 54
Brownian motion, 120–121
Buy-and-hold strategies, 15, 31, 52

Central-limit theorem, 166–168
Classification of hedge funds, 7–12
 by other criteria, 8
 by type of fund, 7–8
 using value-added factor, 9–12, 151–152
Closed-end funds, 83
Closing funds, 127–128
Collateralized loans:
 collateral loan ratio, 73–76
 collateral valuation, 72
 in creating leverage, 67–68
Commodity trading advisers (CTAs), 24
Correlation, 175–177
Correlation coefficient, 176–177

D ratio:
 computation of, 60
 in detecting leverage, 77–78, 83–85
 deviations in, 103–104, 105–107
 distinguishing luck from skill and,
  96–103
 distribution of returns and, 90–93
 of fund versus assets, 77
 and Global Systems Fund, 147
 as indicator of risk, 58–61
 in measuring manager's skills, 60,
  96–104, 105

Derivatives:
 in creating leverage, 69
 in hedging, 2
 nature of, 3
Detecting leverage, 77–85
 d ratio in, 77–78, 83–85
 example, 79–85
 measuring effective use, 78–79
 problems in, 77–78
Directionality, 10
Diversification, 175–177
 correlation and, 175–177
 overdiversification, 132–133
 in risk management, 54
Due-diligence process, 22, 28, 83

Education of a Speculator, The
 (Niederhoffer), 147

Failure of hedge funds, 117–128
 gambler's ruin and, 117–127
 mortality rates, 127–128, 130–131
Fees, 25
Financial risk, 33–48
 characteristics of, 34–35
 complexity of, 35–37
 defined, 33
 dynamic nature of, 35–37, 153
 hidden assumptions in standard
  deviation, 46–48
 problems applying statistical tools to
  hedge funds, 43–46
 problems with statistical measurements
  of, 42–43
 randomness and, 103–104
 rewards and, 34–35
 transfer to third party, 53
 as variability of expected returns, 37–42
Fractal, 129
Funds of funds:
 hidden leverage in, 70
 overleveraging to boost rewards, 63–64
 pro forma returns on, 24

Stefano Lavinio is founder and managing director of Lara Capital Management, a money management and hedge fund firm with more than $250 million under management. A twenty-year veteran of the international financial markets, Lavinio currently manages a series of investment programs and hedge funds, including an international fixed income arbitrage fund that has been consistently rated among the top performers for the last four years. He is a popular speaker at seminars and conferences in both Europe and the United States, is a graduate of the Bocconi University in Milan, Italy, and also holds degrees in economics from Columbia University in New York City.

DATE DUE